W9-BHW-178

"Here is an author who has captured the imagination of the world, and become, perhaps, the most widely read inspirational writer of our time".

The Christian Herald

NORMAN VINCENT PEALE
has inspired millions to achieve success, satisfaction and happiness in life.

In this exciting worldwide bestseller, he demonstrates the power of plus factor in action. A power that can change you dramatically into an entirely new person — one who is stronger, more confident, better balanced, more energetic, more resilient, more capable of coping with the ever-increasing complexity of modern living.

Through the actual experiences of men and women who have reinvented their lives, Dr Peale shows, how you can develop the inner potential of plus factor to transform your life and win success.

**Also in
Orient Paperbacks**

Achieve Success and Happiness
Living with a Purpose
Success is Never Ending, Failure is Never Final!
Tough Times Never Last, But Tough People Do!
Practical Ways to a Powerful Personality

Secrets of Success
Why Some Positive Thinkers Get Powerful Results
Treasury of Courage and Confidence
Sucess in 30 Days
10 Steps to Positive Living

Power of the Plus Factor

NORMAN VINCENT PEALE

Orient
Paperbacks

DELHI | MUMBAI | HYDERABAD

Scripture verses in this book are from the
King James Version of the Bible.

Lines from 'The Quitter' are from *The Collected Poems of
Robert Service,* Dodd, Mead & Company, Inc., publishers.

'Words to Grow on' by Grant Teaff were adapted from
Winning: It's How You Play the Game by Grant Teaff, Word
Books, 1985, and reprinted from *Guideposts* magazine,
September 1986.

The kingdom of God is within you.

Luke 17:21

ISBN : 978-81-222-0310-3

Power of the Plus Factor

Subject: Self Help / Personal Growth / Self Esteem

© 1987 Norman Vincent Peale

1st Published 2002
8th Printing 2014

Published in arrangement with
Fleming H. Revell
(A division of Baker Books Co., USA)

Published by
Orient Paperbacks
(A division of Vision Books Pvt. Ltd.)
5A/8 Ansari Road, New Delhi-110 002
www.orientpaperbacks.com

Cover design by Vision Studio

Printed at
Anand Sons, Delhi-110 092, India

Cover Printed at
Ravindra Printing Press, Delhi-110 006

Contents

1

The Challenge of
the Plus Factor

*W*hat if I were to tell you that there is a power within you that can revolutionize your life.

A power that is invisible, intangible, but completely real.

A power that can transform you so dramatically, that under its influence and guidance you can become an entirely new person, stronger, more confident, better balanced, more energetic, more resilient, more capable of coping with the ever-increasing complexity of modern living.

Suppose I added that this remarkable force could lift you from failure to success, from illness to health, from self-doubt to self-assurance.

And then, if I assured you further that it could help you find congenial friends, solve problems, break out of stale habits, fairly explode into a world totally different from the world you have known before, a world of enthusiasm and exhilaration and understanding and joy—what would your reaction be?

I think you'd want to find out about this power: What is it called? Where does it come from? How do I find it? What must I do to make it operative in my life?

My answers might surprise you because basically they are so simple. Everyone knows that there is a life force that sustains and animates every living thing on this planet of ours. With it, you are alive. Without it, you are dead. This life force was put into all of us by God Himself. What I'm writing about here is a special manifestation of it, a special concentration of it that will do remarkable things for those who understand it and reach for it and allow it to function in their lives.

I call it the Plus Factor.

It's the quality of *extra*-ness that we see in certain people.

People who live with more eagerness, more energy, more enthusiasm than others.

Who set higher goals and achieve them more often.

Who keep going despite adversity and hardship.

Who shrug off misfortune and give out warmth and caring and encouragement wherever they go.

People, in short, who have, in themselves, a marvelous Plus Factor at work.

Well, you may say, I know such people, but what about me? How do I get hold of this extra-ness? Where can I find this Plus Factor?

The answer to that is simple too. You will find it in the last place you might think of: within yourself.

When God fashions a human being like you or me, how does He go about it? I like to think that first He arranges all the intricate parts of the body so that they are in balance and harmony with one another: the skin, the bones, the nerves, all the elements that go into a marvelous machine designed to last a lifetime.

But He, who created us 'a little lower than the angels,' adds one thing more. He gives each of us a power that I call the Plus Factor—that extra something in the spirit.

There it remains, deep in the personality of every individual. You don't have to search for it; it's already there. But there is one thing you must realize about the Plus Factor. Its power is potential, but it is not self-activating. It is latent in human beings and will remain latent until it is activated.

That is why it manifests itself more strongly in some people than in others. They are the people who have learned how to call it forth.

If you want this wonderful stream of power to be activated in you, there are four preliminary things you should do.

❑ First, make the key discovery that the Plus Factor is no myth, no abstraction, but a reality that has been recognized and used by wise men and women for centuries.

❑ Next, you accept the fact that it is already planted inside of you, waiting to be released.

❑ Then you decide you want it to become operative. There can be no maybes, no hesitancies, no half-heartedness about this. You must want it intensely, urgently, ardently. And you must want it *now*.

❑ You decide to face the fact that this marvelous potential built into you is not being fully realized.

You admit that in the past—partly through ignorance—it has been blocked, ignored, neglected. You make a promise to yourself to rearrange your thought patterns so that the blocks are removed, and the power can come surging through.

❑ Finally you do the thing that gives power to your life—the Scripture method, 'To as many as received him, to them gave he the power to become . . .' (see John 1:12).

We live in a universe of laws that operate in the spiritual as well as the physical world. And here is the crucial thing to remember: *The Plus Factor makes its appearance in a person's life in proportion as that person is in harmony with God and His universal laws.*

If you want the Plus Factor to operate in your life, if you want to be on the receiving end of the extra flow of power, you need to learn to think a certain way and act a certain way and be a certain kind of person.

This learning process is well within the reach of all of us, and this book is designed to help you master it. But don't expect that mastery to come easily. The Plus Factor is implanted in all of us. But it is planted deep.

It is almost as if the Creator knew that a degree of struggle is good for His children. He also knew that they value most what they have to work for. Consequently, He arranged things so that the Plus Factor is not going to emerge spontaneously in a person. It has to be understood and activated. The Lord installed this hidden dynamo, but it's our job to remove the blocks and hindrances that short-circuit the emergence of power. It's our job, to open the doors

*You are greater
than
you think you are.*

of our inner selves and let this force, this Plus Factor, come through.

You can often tell at a glance whether the Plus Factor is working in people or not. You see a young woman walking down a city street, bright hair blowing in the wind, an almost tangible aura of health and vitality about her, confidence in her clear eyes, a sense of purpose in her stride, and you say to yourself, 'Yes, there it is. She has it. She has the Plus Factor and the Plus Factor has her.'

Then you come upon some unfortunate derelict slumped against a wall, head sunk on chest, eyes staring vacantly into space, and you know very well that the Plus Factor is not operative. It has been blocked by some or all of a whole series of minus factors: alcohol, drugs, fear, anxiety, guilt, disease, negated to the point where the individual is no longer able to cope with even the most elementary challenge of existence. Or there may be a person of obvious ability who is not living at a level of creativity that his aptitudes indicate he should attain.

I do not believe there is any exact blueprint or precise formula for the release of the Plus Factor. If there were, we would all have it to a far greater extent than we do. But the more we learn to believe in it, trust it, and open ourselves to it, the more we find that goals are achieved, ambitions are realized, high energy levels are maintained, fears and tensions subside, and spiritual growth becomes not just possible but almost inevitable.

In this book I shall indicate some of the key areas of living, and show how the Plus Factor has helped people in times of difficulty or distress, and offer suggestions that will help the reader find it and use

12

it. The purpose of this book is to make possible a better understanding of this inner potential and make it begin to operate in people.

Let's begin where the Plus Factor impinges on an intangible and remarkable aspect of human existence: the area of dreams.

2

Creative Dreaming

*D*o you sometimes feel that you are living below your potential?

Are you ever troubled by the thought that greater energies, more creative ideas, and problem-solving capacities are locked away inside you?

If so, you are not alone. We *all* have such feelings from time to time.

I think such feelings come from an awareness that the life force in each of us is a fraction of the great universal Life Force that we call God. Since we are made in His image, then we should have access to all the power we need to live successfully and triumphantly. The Plus Factor should operate in us, not just now and then, but all the time.

Why don't we have it every minute, every hour? Because we let certain things block it. Ignorance can block it. Fear can block it. Hatred, envy, anger, anxiety, negative thoughts, selfish actions . . . all these things can keep the Plus Factor from functioning. Some of it may get through, enough perhaps to keep us going, barely. But it will be only a trickle instead of the powerful force it is supposed to be.

Fortunately, just as there are attitudes and actions that narrow the flow of power, there are some that widen the channel and let more of the power through. The first step to be taken in order to start the Plus Factor operating is to learn to be a creative dreamer.

When I use the word *dream* the reference is not to those shadowy images that flicker through our minds when we are asleep. No, the dreams I'm writing about are the indistinct hopes, the far-off visions, the first faint stirrings of the imagination that come when we are in the earliest stages of planning something worthwhile. And there's a wonderful thing about such dreams. In some uncanny way that no one fully understands, they seem to contain the seeds of their own fulfilment. If you dream something long enough and hard enough, a door seems to open and through that door come mighty forces that will guide and support you in your efforts to make the dream come true.

Creative dreaming, in other words, activates the release of power that we call the Plus Factor.

Hard-nosed, practical people sometimes scoff at such a notion. To them the term *dreamer* implies vagueness and impracticality.

I remember vividly a conversation I had as a young man with my crusty old Uncle Herschel. He was a top businessman and a pillar of his community, but he could be gruff on occasion.

To get through college I had to borrow money. Since Uncle Herschel was the one member of the family who had any money, I borrowed from him.

Then after college, when I wanted to go to graduate school, I needed more money; so I went to see Uncle Herschel again.

'Uncle Herschel,' I said, 'I know I still owe you some money, but now I'd like to borrow some more.'

Uncle Herschel did not look exactly overjoyed. 'What do you want more for?' he demanded.

'I want to become a minister,' I said. 'The world is full of people who need help. I'd like to do something about people's problems. I have a dream of helping people.'

Uncle Herschel gave a loud snort. 'Dreams!' he said. 'Dreams won't get you anywhere!'

Right behind him on the wall was a framed copy of American Declaration of Independence. I knew he thought a great deal of it, so I pointed to it. 'That was made by dreams,' I told him. 'The men who signed that piece of paper had a dream—a dream of a free nation, under God. That document is the embodiment of their dream. Because they had a dream, you and I are living here in freedom today.'

Uncle Herschel mumbled and grumbled for a while, but he let me have the loan. And I guess he dreamed that I would pay him back, because eventually I did. I cherish the memory of the good man.

The world has always been full of dramatic examples of what can happen when one determined man or woman locks his or her mind around a dream and lets the Plus Factor begin to come through. Almost two centuries ago William Lloyd Garrison was living in a nation where human slavery was accepted as a natural and even desirable state of affairs. But Garrison decided that it was a monstrous crime against God and humanity. He began to dream of a nation where slavery no longer existed. He began to dream that he—one lonely individual—could actually help make this stupendous change come to pass. He said to himself, in this impossible dream, 'I am going to destroy slavery in this land.'

The odds against him were overwhelming. The general assembly of a church had stated that slavery was ordained by God. Prominent statesmen insisted that the whole edifice of America rested on slavery.

Such was the status of slavery in the United States, economically blessed by the North as well as the South, when William Lloyd Garrison dared to dream his dream. But with a tremendous surge of power from the Plus Factor he forged his dream into a 'hammer,' and he pounded it against this great rock of slavery. People jeered and laughed, but year after year Garrison continued to beat with his hammer, until the hammer grew and became a mighty sledge whose thunderings could be heard throughout the land. Finally, a crack appeared in the solid monolith of slavery, and the thrilling fact is that, finally, slavery was outlawed in the United States.

Remember, too, what Martin Luther King said a hundred years later, when he talked of a world in which the remnants of racism and prejudice would be abolished? He said, 'I have a dream . . .'

Dreamers are almost always optimists. A pessimist—someone who sees only negative possibilities—believes that nothing good is likely to happen. But dreamers believe that nothing is too good to be true. They live with excitement, because their dreams help them generate it. My mother was a dreamer: she saw romance and poetry in everything. I remember one foggy night

17

on a Hudson River ferryboat when she spent half an hour trying to make me see and feel the thrill and mystery of great ships passing one another in the darkness, lights glowing dimly, whistles bellowing hoarsely. And I guess she succeeded, because, after all these years I still remember it.

Sometimes that marvelous mechanism, the unconscious mind, will use an actual dream—the kind that comes while we're sleeping—to send a message to someone who has been wrestling with a problem. A few years ago in Texas an unemployed salesman named Jim Head, unable to find a selling job, had been trying to earn a few dollars by making cheese-cakes—his mother had been a notable cook—and selling them to friends. But the income from this fell far short of his needs. Then one night he had an astonishingly 'real' dream in which he saw himself baking a cake, using all sorts of unusual ingredients. So clear was the dream and so detailed the recipe that he even remembered when he woke up how much baking soda he had used.

Amazed by the vividness of this dream sequence, he went into the kitchen, and concocted a cake exactly to the dream specifications. When a neighbor came in later Jim offered him a piece. 'Yahoo!' cried the visitor. 'It's terrific!'

Thus was born the Yahoo cake. Baked in the shape of the Lone Star State, it has sold tremendously. Jim Head had little experience as a baker; he knew nothing about food distribution. But the Plus Factor that came surging in on the heels of that compelling dream gave him the energy and the optimism to overcome all such handicaps and limitations. Today he is a happy and successful man.

Dream the
impossible dream

Don Quixote

Dreams know no boundaries of age or race or nationality. Not long ago in Japan, we were staying in a lovely new hotel on a hillside just outside the center of Tokyo. The management was very kind to me, and so when time came to leave I asked to see the owner to express my thanks. He was a dignified Japanese gentleman at whose hotel in Kyoto I had stayed several times. He was now eighty years old but still full of vitality and animation. I asked him how he came to be in the hotel business, expressing admiration for his enterprise and energy in building and running a big, new hotel at an age when most men would long since have retired.

'Oh,' he said, 'as you know, this is not my only hotel. I have four others. All my life I've dreamed of being a good innkeeper. As a child, I set that goal for myself. I dreamed it would happen. I believed it would happen. And it did happen. To be successful you must first have a dream. Then you must work very hard. Finally, if you dream hard and work hard, the dream comes true. Isn't that so in your country also?'

I assured him that it was. I told him how my friend Bill Marriott, who built a great hotel empire, started with a little root beer stand and no money at all. I also told about another friend, Dave Thomas, the president and founder of Wendy's restaurants, who started out as a dishwasher in Annapolis, but this did not stop him. Why? Because he had a dream—a dream of a restaurant that offered only one item: a superb hamburger. He had the dream and he had the willingness to work, and again, when those two explosive ingredients were mixed together, the Plus Factor was liberated and swept him to astonishing success.

I believe the long dreams we dream as children have a lasting effect upon our lives. Once I asked Dorothy Draper, one of the foremost interior designers in America, to decorate our Institutes of Religion and Health in New York City. Dorothy had a genius for combining colors in a most arresting and dramatic way. She told us that color can either elevate or depress the spirit. So she used bright colors to uplift and stimulate emotions, and soft colors to reduce tension. She also told me that as a little girl, living in poverty in a very plain and drab house, she used to lie in bed and in her mind endow her room with the radiance of all the colors of the spectrum. Her dream was that some day she would lift the spirits of thousands of people everywhere by her infusions of color. And that is exactly what she did.

An example of the Plus Factor in action? She believed it was.

The most memorable song in the musical play *Man of La Mancha* is the one where Don Quixote urges all who will listen to him to 'dream the impossible dream.' It's a song based on the old knight's burning conviction that the Plus Factor will come to the aid of anyone who does. In fact, the more impossible the dream, the promise says, the greater is the power, that will come.

In Chicago years ago there was a ragged newsboy who used to huddle on a sidewalk grating near the Chicago *Tribune* building because the flow of heat from the presses operating in the basement of the building kept him warm. From that vantage point, the boy could see well-dressed men and women going into a theater across the street where brilliant lights on the marquee spelled out the evening's attraction. He decided one cold night that some day he would be that attraction himself, and to record the birth of this impossible dream he took a rusty nail and scratched his name and date on the concrete of a window-sill behind the grating. And the years passed, and the dream did not die, and the day came when the ragged newsboy, now attired in white tie and tails, held the crowds that came to the theater spellbound with the most astounding array of magical tricks the stage had ever seen. He was Howard Thurston, the great magician, and sometimes he would take his friends and show them the name and the date dimly scratched on the concrete window-sill so many years before.

A dream just as impossible as that once came to a little black child living in an orphanage in Troy, New York. Her name was Dorothy Brown. When Dorothy was five years old, she was taken to a hospital for a tonsillectomy. Most youngsters would have been frightened, or at least apprehensive, but Dorothy wasn't. She was fascinated by the wondrous world of medicine in which she found herself. People helping other people by relieving pain, setting broken bones, curing diseases. Then and there, Dorothy Brown decided that some day she would be part of that world. She was only five years old, but she set a goal for herself: Eventually she would become a doctor.

It was a dream that seemed absolutely hopeless. Born out of wedlock, she had been placed in the orphanage because her mother could not afford to keep her. It was understood that when she reached the age when other children enter high school, she would have to go to work. She had no friends outside the orphanage, no family, no connections of any kind. And yet . . .

And yet, something flickered inside this child, a tiny spark that became a flame. A flame that ignored

22

all the odds, all the laws of probability. A flame breathed on by the Plus Factor, and consequently a flame that didn't go out.

One day this little girl, Dorothy Brown, asked the superintendent of the orphanage why she never had any visitors, as some of the other children did. That kind man mentioned this to some of his friends at the church he attended. The result was that a white family named Coffeen came to see the child. When Dorothy told them she intended to be a doctor, they listened and they didn't laugh. They felt her chances were nonexistent, but still they gave her attention and, affection and encouragement.

As was the orphanage custom in those days, at the age of fourteen Dorothy went to work as a maid, earning $14 a week. Two dollars a day. There were many books in her employer's home, and she was allowed to read them. In two years, she saved $500, and decided to register for high school. When the registrar asked for her home address, she had to admit that she had no job, no home, no address.

But when a person has the aura of the Plus Factor about her, other people step forward to help, impelled by impulses that they may or may not understand. The principal of the high school listened to Dorothy's story. Then he found a couple who agreed to take her in as a boarder. She paid for her room as long as her money held out. When it ran out, the couple kept her anyway.

When she graduated from high school, she went back to being a maid in order to earn money for college. At the wages then being paid, she figured it would take her eleven years. But her faith in her dream never faltered. Every night she asked God to help her turn it into a reality. She worked extra hours. She took on extra jobs. Something gave her the endurance and energy she needed. I'm convinced it was the Plus Factor.

One of her employers, hearing her talk of becoming a doctor, told her of a scholarship being offered by a small Methodist college in North Carolina. She applied for that scholarship and won it. She took all the science and pre-med courses that were offered. But when finally she graduated, there was no money for medical school.

When you are really in the flow of the Plus Factor, when its invisible current is supporting and sustaining you, it sometimes seems that even the mighty sweep of world events reaches out to help. The onset of World War II caused a shortage of manpower, and the army turned to women with a background in science to work as inspectors in ordnance depots. In two years, Dorothy Brown saved $2,000. It still wasn't enough, but she could wait no longer. She entered Meharry Medical College in Nashville, Tennessee. When her funds ran out, friends came to her aid. And the day finally came when the friendless little waif from the orphanage in Troy, New York, was a doctor at last.

What does Dr. Brown herself think about all this? She believes quite simply that now she is living the dream that entered her mind when she was five years old. She believes that just as God gives each one of us our special talent, so He gives us dreams to make us aware of that talent. 'It doesn't matter,' she says, 'how far-fetched or unattainable the dream may seem. If we remain steadfast, if we have enough faith in God and in ourselves to go to work and stay at work trying to make the dream come true, then God puts into our lives the people who, out of their love for Him

24

and for us, will do for us what we cannot do for ourselves.'

A dream vividly imagined. A goal tenaciously pursued. A faith that God will help you with a worthy ambition. An unshakable determination to work and work and keep on Working. These are all keys that open the door to the power that we call the Plus Factor.

Dreams are not just idle nothings. They are the parents of possibilities. Possibilities are the descendants of dreams. Without the one, there can never be the other. Dream, therefore. Dream big, dream long, dream strong. And remember . . .

Sometimes the Plus Factor is only a dream away.

3

Setting Goals

*L*et's assume you have begun to liberate the Plus Factor in your nature by the process of creative dreaming.

Now what must you do?

Since the Plus Factor is to function with ever-increasing power, you must work on those dreams.

You need to shape them, focus them, hammer them down to their essence.

You have to build a viaduct over which they can pass from the world of dreams to the world of reality.

In other words, you have to learn to set goals.

Four centuries ago the great French essayist Michel de Montaigne wrote these words: 'No wind favors him who has no destined port.'

He meant that a person without clear-cut goals in life is forever doomed to sail in circles, always frustrated, always rudderless, never getting anywhere.

Montaigne's words were true then and perhaps they're even more true today, because the world has become a more complex and competitive place. In this fast-moving, super-specialized century, unless you are able clearly and calmly and deliberately to set goals for yourself, you are becalmed in indecision and inertia.

When people set goals for themselves that are clear and distinct; when they hold tenaciously to those goals through times of disappointment, frustration, or even apparent failure; when they image themselves progressing steadily toward those goals and finally achieving them, then a force emerges from deep within them so powerful that it is virtually irresistable. That is the Plus Factor.

Once the Plus Factor makes its appearance and really takes hold, the surge of energy and confidence becomes so strong that it overcomes all obstacles. Let me give you an example from a small farming community in eastern Pennsylvania.

Walter Harter, just graduated from high school in that small town, seemed like quite an ordinary young man. He had a slight limp caused by a badly broken leg in childhood. Otherwise he seemed like an average young fellow, unable to go to college because his family couldn't afford it.

As any farmer can tell you today, things can get very tough in a farming community. Certainly there were few openings for any kind of work in Walter Harter's area. But a dream and a plan had been stirring in the back of this young man's mind. And when a dream and a plan get together, the result can be a goal . . . sometimes a goal that opens the door to the Plus Factor.

In Walter Harter's case, the goal was to find work in New York City, which he had never visited, and where he didn't know a soul. Only one thing could have given him the unshakable conviction that he could achieve such a goal: the Plus Factor within.

Walter Harter went to the local telephone office and borrowed the New York City telephone directory. He looked up the listings of various stores in the metropolitan area. Finally he decided to concentrate on a well-known chain of stores. There were addresses for 393 of them scattered over Manhattan, Brooklyn, Queens, Long Island, and the Bronx. Walter Harter told himself that among all those stores there had to be an opening for him. He made up his mind to write a letter to every single one of them.

This was a big undertaking for a teenager with no resources, no help of any kind. He composed a letter expressing his desire to become associated with any store in the chain in any capacity from floor sweeper on up. He had no typewriter so wrote by hand to 393 managers of the various stores. He set himself a quota of fifteen letters a day, and he stuck to it, day after day.

No replies came back. Not a single one. Of all the various forms of rejection, silence can be the most devastating. But something was pushing—and sustaining—Walter Harter. He kept doggedly on.

Finally, Walter Harter asked his parents to let him leave home and try his luck in the Big City. They were apprehensive because he knew no one there. But they agreed to let him go and scraped up enough money to sustain him for a few days. They figured he'd be back soon.

In Manhattan, Walter went to Times Square and there found one of the chain's large stores. He asked for the manager, who explained that even if the store had received a letter from Walter, it would have been sent to the personnel department of the chain.

Walter wasn't even sure what a personnel department was, but he followed directions to a huge building on Park Avenue. There, when he identified himself, he was taken to a stern-faced man behind an enormous desk who seemed to be in charge of everything. The man stared at Walter for what seemed like a long time. Finally he stood up, smiled, and pointed to a table holding stacks of letters. 'Your applications are there,' he said, 'all three hundred and ninety-three of them! We knew that some day you would walk in here. We have a clerk's job waiting for you. You can start this afternoon.'

An amazing story? Yes, but a true one. Walter Harter eventually became a store manager. And even after he moved on to other things, he carried with him the momentum that the Plus Factor, in the form of initiative and perseverance, had given him.

This process of aligning yourself with the inner flow of power and becoming a true goal setter isn't easy. Like any other skill, it has to be studied and practiced before it can be mastered. It comes by developing a positive attitude and imposing certain disciplines on yourself. If you are suffering from aimlessness and a sense of defeat, especially negativism, here are five suggestions that will help you. I know, for at different times in my own life they have helped me.

One: Sharpen your thinking about goal setting.

Give it some real thought. Obviously, goals range all the way from very broad life goals to small specific goals. Learn to distinguish between long-term and short-term goals. Decide how many you can handle.

Be realistic about the amount of time and effort that may be necessary. The objective is worth the price. One must not drift in vague circles but use the compass of the brain, and chart a course, and follow it.

Two: Make a commitment to excellence.

Sometimes people say, 'Well, I really don't know yet what I want to do with my life.' Okay, perhaps not. But while you're waiting for that goal to come into view, or into focus, there is nothing to stop you from choosing one supremely important goal: the determination to do *everything* as well as you can, to make the most of whatever the Lord put into you in the way of talent or ability.

A few years ago, I remember, I met a lady who had been in high school with me. She looked at me pensively for quite a while. Finally she said, 'Well, I guess you've done pretty well with what little you had!' People always laugh when I tell this story, but in a way she was paying me a great compliment. At least, I like to think so. I hope I took that little and tried to make the most of it. That is what we are supposed to do.

Actually, my long-term goal in life has been a clear and direct one ever since I left the newspaper business many years ago to enter the ministry. That goal is to persuade the greatest possible number of people to commit their lives to God. To get people to know that He is just as alive today as He was two thousand years ago in Judea and Galilee. That He can bring peace and power into their lives. That is my goal today and for as long as I live. I have pursued it with every ounce of determination and energy that I possess. More than once I have run into difficulties. But always the Plus Factor has come to my aid and pulled me through dark periods.

No wind favors him who has no destined port

Michel De Mountaigue
(16th Century French Essayist)

Three: Learn to distinguish between a goal and a wish.

There's an old saying, 'If wishes were horses, beggars would ride.' That's just a way of saying that simply wishing for something isn't going to make it happen. The fairy tales we all loved as children are full of spells that bring instant happiness and charms that make dreams come true; but they are fantasy, not reality. The reason such stories have had such appeal through the ages is that they promise glowing rewards without effort. Life isn't like that.

Quite often, I think, people cling to wishes that are really just fantasies. I used to stay sometimes at a certain hotel in the Midwest. Whenever I did the young manager always assured me that his ambition was to become governor of that particular state. He was an affable and likable fellow, and he met a lot of people in his role of innkeeper. But nothing ever happened to change his way of life.

I finally discovered that this ambition of his dated from the time when the governor had stayed at the hotel. All the pomp and ceremony surrounding him impressed the manager a great deal, and he decided that it would be nice to be governor himself some day. This concept made him feel important, so he clung to it, magnified it, talked about it. But it was just a wish, a daydream akin to the vision I used to have as a small boy when, growing up in Ohio, I dreamed of playing shortstop for the Cincinnati Reds. It was a glorious idea, but it was just a wish and so not a realizable goal.

Compare the daydreaming hotel manager with a young couple I knew who wanted a home of their own. They couldn't afford to buy a house, but they did manage a down payment on a lot. Once they had the lot, they drew some rough plans on wrapping paper on the kitchen table of their little rented apartment. Then they went out with stakes and string and paced off an outline of their dream house on the lot. They discussed what every room would contain, what it would look like. Whenever they wanted more of a house they would change the stakes and the string. This went on month after month.

In the meantime, they set themselves the discipline of a double tithe. Both had jobs. They set aside 10 per cent of their joint earnings for their church, and another 10 per cent for their 'some day' house, if either of them took a moonlighting job, that money went into their building fund. They denied themselves a lot of minor pleasures to keep the fund growing.

At the end of three years they took their plans and their savings to a mortgage company. By this time there was a kind of momentum, a quiet confidence, an aura of determination about them that impressed even the hard-boiled loan officer. Call it the Plus Factor, call it what you will, they got their mortgage, they built their dream house, they're living happily in it today with two attractive children.

Why? Because they didn't sit and vaguely wish. They had a definite plan. They had a timetable. They had a goal, and they went for it, and they got it.

Four: Prepare for ultimate goals by achieving interim goals.

If you learn to do this consistently, you won't even have to overtax yourself for your ultimate goals; they will come to you in due course.

Often I've seen this happen in industry. Once I asked a bank president how he got his start in banking. 'By cleaning things,' he said with a smile. 'My first job was sweeping up in a little small-town bank. It wasn't much of a job, but I cleaned everything as if my whole future in banking depended on it. Which of course, at that point, it did.

'Finally, I became an errand boy, then a teller, then a cashier, and so on. At every stage, I tried to do everything well. By the time they needed a president to clean up some really big financial problems, I knew every step of the banking business. And so they called on me.' That man rose from a menial position to a top post, and I have no doubt that the Plus Factor was aiding him all the way.

The principle involved here is completely logical and completely sound: The training and experience you acquire in attaining a lesser goal leaves you ready to pursue a greater one. I knew a young man once who had considerable potential as a writer. His long-range goal was to be a novelist, but he knew that called for more maturity and more craftsmanship than he had. So he set himself a progression of separate but related goals. He got a job on a magazine that enabled him to observe how short stories were constructed, why some were successful and others were not. Then he became a writer of short stories himself. Next, he became associated with a television network and learned how dramatic scripts were put together. Finally he did begin to write novels and, not instantly but eventually, met with considerable success. Why? Because he didn't leap for a goal, he worked toward it; he prepared himself step-by-step for success. Then he was ready.

Five: Choose goals that will benefit others as well as yourself.

A goal that involves concern for other people seems to liberate the Plus Factor much more readily than one that doesn't. It's not enough for a person entering medical school to want to be rich and successful; his or her basic goal should be the desire to help people. The same is true of lawyers, businessmen, or whomever. You'll find it helps to have the concept of service embedded in the goal.

I once asked John Johnson, publisher of *Ebony* magazine, the secret of his great success. 'By small realizable goals,' he replied. 'In time they added up to the achievement of big goals.'

This is the attitude that underlies some of America's greatest success stories. A number of years ago, a young man, the son of a midwestern college president and preacher, was flailing around at various jobs; his problem: 'None of them really seemed to serve anyone.' Since childhood he had been imbued with the Christian ethic, which involved, among other things, the concept of service, of the improvability of the individual, the value of time, the importance of attitude. Even as a seventeen-year-old, he had begun the habit of writing on slips of paper the gist of his daily reading in magazines and books; just before sleep he would repeat what he had learned that day, referring to his slips of paper if he forgot anything.

Finally, in 1921, pushed out of his job at Westinghouse in Pittsburgh because of a recession, he decided to push ahead with his idea that had been born of that early reading: to publish a Reader's Service, consisting of articles of value, condensed to save time, and issued in a small, pocket-sized magazine that the reader could carry around and refer to at odd moments. Then the young man had approached existing magazine publishers of the time; they had all turned down his idea. Even the great William Randolph Hearst told him it would never sell enough to succeed. But, as the young man said some years later, 'I didn't care if I made a penny, as long as the magazine served the reader.'

Already the Plus Factor that comes to the aid of people with altruistic goals was coming into the picture. With faith in his idea, DeWitt Wallace and his wife, Lila, started putting out their little magazine. That was in 1922. When the Wallaces died, the little magazine had 100 million readers, 30 million subscribers, 18 million in the United States and the rest worldwide. The *Reader's Digest* was, and is, the great publishing success story of our time.

I knew the Wallaces well, and whenever I was with them the focus of the conversation always was, 'How can we help young people? How can we help older people? How can we help anyone anywhere who needs help?'

So if you have a goal that includes helping people in some way, don't let anyone talk you out of it. Don't believe them when they say, 'It can't be done.' Miracles can happen when you set clear, worthwhile, useful goals and go after them with belief. So aim high. Put all negative or defeatist thoughts out of your mind, and give it all you've got. When you do, great forces will come to your aid.

Among them will be your inner Plus Factor.

4
Two Magic Words

*W*e have written about the importance of creative dreaming. We have stressed the necessity of setting goals.

Is there a logical third step in this process of liberating and activating the Plus Factor in human beings?

Yes, there is. It consists of just two magic words.

Let me digress for a moment. Have you ever thought about the power inherent in certain combinations of words? Shakespeare tells in ten words how a person's future is determined: 'To be or not to be; that is the question.' Of course it's the question! Is the Plus Factor to be a force in your life, or is it not? Are you going to set goals and reach them, or are you not? Is success something you will achieve, or isn't it? Is happiness going to come to you, or will it ever remain just beyond your grasp? Are these things to be, or are they not; that is indeed the question.

Then there is an even shorter combination of words than that given by Shakespeare. These words are credited to Henry Kaiser, the great industrialist, and they accurately describe many successful enterprises. Just six words: 'Find a need and fill it.'

And now we get down to two magic words that tell us how to accomplish just about anything we want to accomplish, two powerful words that can change any situation, two dynamic words that all too few people use. And what are these two amazing words?

Do it!

Are you defeated by something? Are you afraid of something? Are you hesitant to try something? Many people spend their lives being afraid to do what they really want to do. But if they stand tall and say, 'I will do this thing!' then the Plus Factor is liberated and power begins to surge into them.

That power begins to flow at the moment one takes the first step or even when the first positive thought comes. No matter how intense your dreaming, no matter how clearly defined your goals, nothing is going to happen until you *make* it happen by taking an active step toward the fulfilment of those dreams, a decisive step toward the realization of those goals.

Back in 1912 when Juliette Low returned from England to her hometown of Savannah, Georgia, she brought with her a dream, a spark of an idea that had been planted by Sir Robert Baden-Powell, the British hero of the Boer War, who had started an organization in England called the Boy Scouts. If scouting was good for the boys of England, Juliette Low asked herself, why wouldn't it be good for the girls of her country? A dream, you see; a creative dream. All the way across the Atlantic she thought about the dream and shaped it and honed it until it became a goal, a difficult far-off goal, but still a goal.

❧

Have you got an idea?
Do it!

Do you have a dream?
Do it!

Do you have an
ambition?
Do it!

Have you some
great impulse,
some burning desire?
Do it!

❧

With that dream and that goal in her mind she went back to the town where she was born and called her friend Nina Pape, who was headmistress of a local school.

'Nina,' she said, 'come right over. I've got something for the girls of Savannah and the girls of Georgia and the girls of the whole country and the whole world *and we're going to start it tonight!'*

There it was, that crucial third step. And as millions of Girl Scouts past and present can testify, they *did it.* It took many years before Girl Scouting became a great national movement, but as the old Chinese proverb says, the longest journey begins with a single step.

I have seen that single step summon the Plus Factor so powerfully that the person taking it was released from a paralysis of fear. Emerson said, 'Do the thing you fear, and the death of fear is certain.' I thought of that prophecy a number of years ago when United States Senator Warren Barbour of New Jersey became a friend of mine. We first met one night at a banquet in Newark where we both were speakers. We sat next to each other at the speakers' table, and he said to me, 'How do you feel when you are about to make a speech? Are you ever scared?'

I admitted to him that often I was, but I'm sure that most public speakers never overcome a certain fear of facing an audience. Maybe that's a good thing, because the adrenaline keys you up and makes your mind work a little better.

Senator Barbour told me that there had been a time when public speaking was sheer agony for him. 'I used to be an amateur boxer,' he said, 'and I was never afraid of anyone in the ring. But when I got up to make a speech my mouth got dry, my hands shook, I went hot and cold all over. Finally I decided I wasn't going to live with a fear like that. So to overcome it I announced my candidacy for the Senate.' (He *did* it.) 'I announced with no idea that I would win, really, but I knew that running for office would force me to go out and make speeches. The only way I could overcome this fear of speaking was to do it.'

So what are you afraid of? What is holding you back? What is it that stands in your way? Do it! I have seen this simple rule work so many times. When I persuade someone to do it they become victorious instead of defeated.

Usually it is fear of failure that is blocking the flow of power from the Plus Factor. That fear leads to inertia, sometimes to a real paralysis of the personality. And the longer the inertia persists, the harder it is to break through it.

Sometimes it can be literally a matter of life or death. I remember an incident that took place a few years ago in North Carolina. A young man named Samuel A. Mann was tramping through the countryside and decided to go through a swamp rather than make a wide detour. He had on high hip boots and was slogging through the wet ground when he came to what looked like an area of dry sand. As he tried to cross it, suddenly he sank down to his knees; and as he tried to get back, a powerful suction gripped his legs like a vise, dragging him down deeper. In a moment of complete horror he realized he was in a great pocket of quicksand and he remembered that the natives always said, 'Nobody ever gets out of those quicksands alive.'

For a moment he was paralyzed by panic, sinking deeper and deeper. To his left he saw some marsh grass

41

growing, each blade perhaps half an inch wide. He thought to himself, 'If I could just reach that grass, perhaps a handful would have the strength of a rope.' He reached out his hand, but there was a gap of about three feet between his fingers and the marsh grass. He knew that if he lunged for the grass and missed it, he would disappear under the treacherous sand. But if he did nothing he was doomed also.

By now the sand was almost over the top of his hip boots, and he realized suddenly that the sand wasn't holding him but rather was holding his boots, which in turn were holding him. With shaking fingers he undid the straps that were holding his boots to his belt. Then, taking a deep breath and asking God to help him, he *did it*. He flung himself full length across the deadly sand. His fingers touched the marsh grass, grasped several strands. Then slowly, carefully, inch by agonizing inch, he pulled himself out of his boots onto the solid earth.

He saved himself because he *did it*.

Do you want power in you? Do you want peace in mind and heart? Do you want to reach for success across the quicksand of timidity and doubt? Then take these two magic words, say them to yourself again and again. Ask God to help you—and DO IT. And not tomorrow or next week or next month or next year.

Now. Do it now!

5

Persisting With the Plus Factor

*I*n the pages of this book so far I have suggested methods to activate the Plus Factor . . .

❑ *Dream creative dreams.*

❑ *Set high and worthwhile goals.*

❑ *Take the first decisive step toward your goal.*

❑ And then what?

Then take another step, and another, and another, until the goal is reached, the ambition realized, the mission accomplished.

No matter how long it takes, *persist.* No matter how discouraged you may get, *persevere.* No matter how much you want to quit, *hang in there.*

President Calvin Coolidge, known widely as 'Silent Cal,' may not have talked a lot, but when he did say something it was usually worth listening to. Here's what he said on this subject:

> Nothing in the world can take the place of persistence. Talent will not; nothing is more common than unsuccessful men with talent.

Genius will not; the world is full of educated derelicts. Persistence and determination alone are omnipotent. The slogan 'press on' has solved and always will solve the problems of the human race.

Winston Churchill said the same thing in different words. Where any worthwhile endeavor was concerned, he said: 'Never give up. Never, never, never . . . give up!'

Why is persistence, why is perseverance of such enormous importance? Because so little of consequence is achieved without it. And because lack of it leads so often to failure. We've all heard the story of the rusty old pickaxe stuck in the rocky wall of an unproductive mine, left there by a miner who had given up in disgust and walked away from it. Years later, another miner idly swung his pick against the same wall and broke through into the fabulous Comstock lode. Untold wealth had been waiting for the first miner if only he had persisted a little longer. A few more swings of the pickaxe would have done it. But he gave up too soon . . . and never knew what that negative decision had cost him.

Contrast that with the job-hunting young man in Boston who saw a want ad in the local paper. He wrote to the post office box number that was given, but received no reply. He wrote again, and yet a third time. Still no answer. So he went to the post office, located the box, and waited until someone came to collect the mail. He followed that person to an office, went inside, and told the office manager what he had done, adding that he still wanted very much to have the job that had been advertised. The manager looked at him in

No matter how long it
takes, 'persist'.
No matter how
discouraged
you may get, 'persevere'.
No matter how much you
want to quit,
'hang in there'.

astonishment. 'Well,' he said, 'we are always looking for people with perseverance and determination. You seem to have both; we'll take you on.' That was how Roger Babson, who later became a famous financier, got his first job.

Sometimes we see people persevering in the face of what seem to be insuperable odds. When that happens, I can't help but think that through their Plus Factor information has been conveyed to them that even they are unaware of.

One of the most remarkable men I ever met was a native of Lebanon, Musa Alami. He had been educated in England, and his family had been quite well off until in one of the disturbances that periodically convulse Lebanon they lost everything. Musa Alami found his way to the bleak desert country of the Jordan River valley not far from Jericho.

This sun-scorched land had probably not changed much since the days of John the Baptist. No crops could grow because of lack of water. There were no funds or equipment to dam the River Jordan. But somehow Musa Alami, who had read of successful irrigation in other areas using subsurface water, became convinced that there might be water underneath the burning sands. And he announced that he was going to dig for it.

Jeers and scornful laughter greeted this announcement. The old Bedouins of the area pointed out that the desert had been there from time immemorial. The water of the Dead Sea had once covered the region; the sand itself was full of salt. Musa Alami was a fool, or perhaps a madman. And it wasn't only the Bedouins who laughed. Government officials and scientists from abroad were equally scornful. No water was there. No water could be there.

Nevertheless, aided by a few poverty-stricken refugees from the nearby Jericho refugee camp, Musa Alami started to dig.

With well-drilling equipment? With steam shovel or earth removers? No. He and his motley crew dug by hand, with pick and shovel. Down they went under the blazing sun. Day after day. Deeper and deeper, while onlookers jeered. Down they went, this dauntless man and his ragged friends, week after week.

What kept them going? Hope kept them going. And with hope they had perseverance, just plain persistence.

I'm sure it came from the Plus Factor.

One day, six months after they started digging, the sand became damp. And a little deeper it was wet. Finally water, fresh water, began to fill the hole. And Musa Alami and his friends did not laugh or shout or cheer. They wept. An ancient Bedouin man said, 'Musa, now I can die. I've seen water come from the desert.'

That's quite a story, isn't it? I know it's true because I knew Musa personally and saw the great stream of water gushing out of the parched heart of the desert. Today thousands of acres are yielding fruits and vegetables of all kinds . . . all because one persistent and determined man was convinced it could happen . . . convinced and sustained by his Plus Factor.

Some years ago in Dallas, Texas, before the Salk vaccine was available, a young man named James C. McCormick was stricken with polio. He was totally paralyzed, totally helpless, and in great pain. He could not move; he could not swallow; he could not breathe; he had to stay in an iron lung. He wanted to die. He prayed, saying, 'Lord, I'm so helpless that I can't take my own life. Please take it for me.'

But God chose to ignore that prayer.

Then he prayed, 'If I can't die, please take away this awful pain.'

The doctors gave him drugs that did ease the pain, but he was becoming dangerously dependent on them.

So he prayed, 'Lord, please take away this craving for drugs.'

And gradually the craving left him.

Then he prayed, 'Please let me be able to swallow again. Let them take this tube out of my throat and these needles out of my arms. If I can just drink a swallow of water, I'll try not to ask for any more favors.'

And he became able to swallow, but he was not able to stop, asking God for favors. The Plus Factor wouldn't let him.

So he prayed, 'Lord, let me be able to breathe a little bit on my own. Let me be able to get out of this iron lung just for a little while.'

And this too came to pass.

After a while he prayed again, 'Heavenly Father, I'm so grateful for all Your favors. Can I ask just one more? Let me be able to leave this bed just for an hour and go in a wheelchair to see the world that lies outside this hospital room.'

This request, too, was granted. Then James McCormick asked to be given strength enough in his arms to move the wheelchair himself. And after that he asked for the ability and stamina to walk on crutches.

And finally, after a twenty-year struggle, James McCormick could walk with two canes, and he was able to marry and have children and lead a very-close-to-normal life.

What did it? The doctors helped. But, supremely, prayer did it—and persistence. But it was prayer of the most intense and most persistent kind. I'm sure that God is not annoyed by such prayers. He doesn't grow impatient or weary of hearing them. His great compassionate heart is touched by such faith and such perseverance. Ask James C. McCormick. He'll tell you the same thing.

Here's how my dictionary defines these two important words:

Persist: To continue steadily and firmly in some state, purpose, or course of action, especially in spite of opposition, remonstrance, etc.

Persevere: To persist in any undertaking, maintain a purpose in spite of difficulty or obstacles, continue steadfastly.

Note that last phrase: *continue steadfastly.* It makes me think of an Ohio housewife and mother named Alice Vonk. She lived in a small town in that rich farming country, and she loved to plant things, especially flowers. She had a little private custom that she always observed. Whenever she put a seed into the ground, she would murmur a little prayer. She figured that human beings could plant the seeds, but it took God to make them grow.

One night Alice Vonk read in a seed catalogue about a prize being offered for a pure white marigold. She loved to grow marigolds herself, but they were always yellow or orange or rust colored. The seed company wanted a pure white marigold because that would enable them to develop hybrids of many colors through cross-pollination, and they were offering a prize of $10,000.

Now Alice Vonk, mother of eight, was no expert on flowers, but she did know a little about hybrids, and something inside her said, 'Why not try it?' She was impelled into action by her Plus Factor.

So Alice Vonk started out with the largest yellow marigolds that she could find in the seed catalogue. As was her custom, she said a little prayer as she dropped each seed into the rich soil. Then she waited.

Finally up came the marigolds, yellow as sunlight. Alice Vonk chose the palest ones, let them die naturally, gathered the seeds and planted them again the next year. 'Somewhere,' she told her skeptical family, 'is a pure white marigold and I am going to find it!' No discouragement there, you see; no doubts, no hint of failure. She was going to persist. She was going to persevere. No matter how long it might take.

And she did, year after year after year. Gradually her marigolds grew paler and paler, but none was the pure white marigold she was seeking. Her children grew up, some of them married and moved away. Her husband died, and for a little while Alice Vonk gave in to sorrow. But then she took a deep breath and went back to her marigolds. By now the grandchildren were coming along, and they were eager to help her. 'Flowers and children are a lot alike,' she said. 'You have to understand them—and never give up on them.'

For almost twenty years she kept planting and praying, always persisting. And then one morning she looked out at her garden and saw, in full glorious bloom, a pure white marigold! Not almost white. Not nearly white. Pure white!

Alice Vonk sent 100 seeds from this marigold to the seed company. There was a long wait while the seeds were tested and grown under laboratory conditions. The day came when the president of the seed company called on the telephone. 'Mrs. Vonk,' he said, 'I'm happy to tell you that you have won our prize!'

And indeed she had.

What was the inner voice that said to Mrs. Vonk, 'Why not try?' What kept her going year after year when most people would have become discouraged and given up? I can only believe that it was the quality we have been writing about all through this book. It was her Plus Factor at work.

Does this unseen quality, the Plus Factor, activate and strengthen the capacity for persistence in a person, or does a display of perseverance in an individual call it forth? I think it probably works both ways. If you make a determined effort on your own, the Plus Factor will come to your aid. On the other hand, there seem to be times when the Plus Factor is manifested in a most unlikely way. It causes that person to choose an almost unattainable goal, and persist against almost insuperable odds until a hopeless hope becomes an actual reality.

Do not minimize the power of persistence. Just hang in there always, always. And never, never give up. Realization and achievement come to those who persist.

'If ye have faith . . . nothing shall be impossible unto you.' The Plus Factor is a reflection of eternal truth.

6

The Plus Factor:
Making it Work

*D*oes one always know when the power of the Plus Factor begins to work? No, not necessarily. Sometime ago I watched on television as Boris Becker, the brilliant young German tennis player, defeated Ivan Lendl in the finals at Wimbledon. Boris and Ivan put on a tremendous match, but there was no doubt as to who was superior that day. The eighteen-year-old youngster with the carrot-colored hair defeated the world's number-one player in straight sets. Lendl, of course, played well, but Becker was in control, and you could tell that Lendl knew it.

Afterward a reporter was asking Becker the usual post-match questions, and the young man was replying with suitable modesty. No, he said, he didn't consider himself the best player in the world. The best on grass, maybe, but not necessarily on slower surfaces.

'You played with great confidence,' the reporter said, 'almost as if you felt you owned the center court at Wimbledon. Is that right?'

Becker nodded slowly, a serious look on his boyish face. 'When I came out to play my very first match in this tournament on this court, I had a strange sensation. It's hard to describe. I felt it in my feet and in my ankles and in my legs . . . . It gave me a great feeling of confidence and strength. I was sure that on this particular court I would go all the way. I was sure that I would win.'

A strange sensation? Almost indescribable? A tremendous feeling of power and assurance?

Was it an expression of the Plus Factor? Who's to say that it wasn't?

Hearing Boris Becker describe the strange feeling that came to him on a tennis court reminded me of a story Michael Landon tells about himself. Today Michael Landon, a television superstar, is famous for his roles in *Bonanza, Little House on the Prairie,* and *Highway to Heaven;* but in those days he was a scrawny tenth grader in New Jersey named Eugene Orowitz . . . called Ugy by his friends.

Ugy was not a good athlete; he was shy and self-conscious. He had no confidence at all until one day, when he was watching some older boys throw the javelin, the coach half-jokingly asked him if he'd like to try. To the amazement of everyone, when Ugy did try, the javelin soared all the way into the grandstand, where it came to rest with a broken point. The coach told the boy he could keep the broken javelin, and from that moment on he began to practice day and night. Before he left high school he had thrown the javelin 211 yards, a national record that year for high school students. His skill brought him a college track scholarship in California, and he thought seriously about the Olympics. As it turned out, a torn muscle in his shoulder eventually put an end to his javelin-throwing career.

But he never forgot the strange feeling that came to him the first time he ever held a javelin in his hand. 'I felt like a Spartan warrior. I had this terrific sense of excitement and confidence and power. It was amazing. And then, years later the same feeling came to me in another area altogether. My javelin-throwing career was over; I was just getting by with odd jobs when a friend of mine who had a part in a play called *Home of the Brave* asked me to rehearse his lines with him. We started reading the script together, and all of a sudden the same sense of excitement and confidence and *rightness* came to me, I knew I wanted to get into dramatics. I knew I wanted to be an actor. I knew I was *supposed* to be an actor. So I enrolled in acting school at Warner Brothers and was on my way.'

How did Michael Landon know he was supposed to be a javelin thrower? How did he know he was supposed to be an actor? Something spoke to him, something deep inside. I think it was the Plus Factor.

Or consider another man, John Holmes, who wrote to me from England. He told me about himself and his childhood in Australia. His parents were farmers who suffered considerably during the Great Depression. 'I was not aware of this as a child,' he wrote, 'because I had space and freedom, care and attention from loving parents.' But life was hard there in the Australian outback.

Gradually it improved so that eventually John was able to borrow some money, buy a small farm of his own, marry, and start raising a family. By the early 1960s, he wrote, things were going pretty well and the Holmeses seemed to have everything they needed.

'But from time to time vague inner stirrings disturbed me. It was like a distant voice telling me there was a bigger and better life for me somewhere. But I ignored it as just a dream.'

Children were born. The 'something' continued to agitate John's mind, kept on whispering that somewhere great things awaited him. But he didn't know what— or where—those things could be.

'By the end of the 1960s I had decided that I must seek opportunities elsewhere. If such opportunities were not to be found, I could always return to what I knew best: farming the land. In 1970 I sold most of the property I owned, settled my debts, which were considerable, and with my wife and children set sail for England. We had no idea where we were going to stay or what we were going to do.'

Now, on the face of it, this was madness. To travel thousands of miles, with few or no resources, to an unfamiliar land where he had no friend or contacts, with five dependents, with no experience or skills except farming . . . one might well say to John Holmes, 'What on earth possessed you?'

The only answer that makes any sense at all is one that would never have occurred to John. It was the Plus Factor that was motivating him, like a whisper in his ear for all those years. The Plus Factor that impelled him to leave his native land and go far across the sea. And it was the Plus Factor, springing from some deep reservoir inside him, that was going to provide him with the energy and the determination to overcome whatever obstacles stood in his way.

'Although it took us more than four weeks to reach England, within ten days of our arrival I had acquired a position as a salesman. I tackled my task with great determination and enthusiasm. My new trade was learned, often with great difficulty, but with the sincere belief that I would eventually succeed."

Well, succeed he did, so much so that today his business firm has franchises in several cities.

Sometimes, I think, a single action on the part of an individual can open the door to the Plus Factor. The long-term results of the action may not be fully apparent for years, but the process has begun.

Consider the case of a young immigrant, Bernard Castro, who came to this country from his native Sicily while still in his teens. Go back through the years to the night when he stood at the grimy window of his cheap room on New York's East Side, staring at the snow that was whirling down, blanketing everything. Already it was a foot deep in the streets; traffic had come to a complete halt.

Still struggling to learn English, young Bernard Castro had signed up for a night course at DeWitt Clinton High School. But that was far away on the other side of the city. Outside the wind howled; the storm was reaching blizzard proportions. Should he try to fight his way through on foot, or should he stay where he was?

Young Castro had found a job as an upholsterer. It paid very little. His mouth was sore from holding the tacks that he hammered into furniture all day long. He was tired, his shoes were thin and his overcoat was thinner. Would it make much difference if he missed one evening's classes?

Standing there before the window Bernard Castro remembered something he had read in a newspaper column. The columnist had said that the margin between success and failure was often simply the willingness to make the extra effort, go the extra mile, endure the extra hardship. Either you had this quality, the columnist said, or you didn't. Abruptly Bernard Castro turned from the window, picked up his shabby overcoat, and plunged into the storm.

On he plodded through the dark, block after block, hands and feet growing numb, until finally he came to the high school entrance—and found it locked. A custodian peered out at him. 'Are you crazy? No one's going to come out on a night like this! The school is closed!' And the door swung shut.

Back through the storm went Bernard Castro, chilled to the bone, head bowed against the icy wind. But as he walked, he felt a little spark of warmth begin to glow inside him. It was the knowledge that out of two thousand students he was the only one who had fought his way to the entrance. He was the only one who had made the extra effort, who had gone the extra mile, and even though his effort was unsuccessful, he knew that the invisible power that had impelled him to make it would support and sustain him in all future endeavors.

He did not know what to call this power; he did not know where it came from. But when at last he came to his little room and fell into his narrow bed, he knew that the force would never desert him—and it never did.

It was the Plus Factor.

Later on Bernard Castro's energy and determination carried him through the Great Depression. He advanced from being an apprentice upholsterer to opening his own interior-decorating business. Nothing very remarkable, you may say—lots of people weathered the Depression. But the mysterious force that led young

Bernard Castro to plow through the blizzard that bitter night continued to guide and influence his life as the years went by.

One gift that the Plus Factor brings out sometimes—and a very valuable gift it is—is the ability to see the hidden potential in apparently unrelated things. Sometimes it's a new use for a familiar object. Sometimes it's a hitherto untried combination of ideas or theories. Sometimes it's the unexpected answer to a puzzling problem.

The time came in Bernard Castro's life when he needed this gift. He was struggling to design a streamlined sofa bed, something slimmer and more attractive than the clumsy davenports that took up so much room. There seemed to be no solution. Nothing worked.

Then one day on a small cabin cruiser Castro watched the owner convert a seat into a bunk by sliding out the lower part of the seat frame and putting cushions down flat. The frame consisted of slats that fitted together like the teeth of two combs. Open, it could sustain the weight of a sleeper. Closed, it took up half the space. There, staring him in the face, was the answer to the design problem that had been baffling Bernard Castro. Using it he designed the Castro convertible sofa bed that made him famous—and rich.

Luck? Alertness? Imagination? Inventiveness?

Yes, certainly, all of these. But when you put them all together, when you add them all up, I think you have to look for something deeper.

You have to credit the Plus Factor, plus stick-to-it-iveness, hard work, hard thinking, and a powerful lot of faith.

7

You Can, If You Think You Can!

hinking back to my school days there is one experience I shall never forget. In the fifth grade I had a teacher who was a confirmed positive thinker. His name was George Reeves and he made an unforgettable impression on his students. He stood over six feet and weighed more than 200 pounds, a towering man.

George Reeves was somewhat of a character, full of vitality, often doing things that were entirely unpredictable. For instance, he had a habit of suddenly shouting, 'Silence!' And believe me, when he demanded silence, there was silence! Then he would go to the blackboard and in big letters print the word C A N' T.

'Look at that word,' he demanded. 'What shall we do with it?'

We knew the answer he wanted and the whole class would chant: 'Knock the T off the CAN'T.' And with a sweeping gesture, George Reeves would erase the T, leaving the word CAN standing out impressively. Dusting the chalk from his hands, he would face us. 'Let that be a lesson to you and never forget it. You *can* if you think you can.' Glaring at the boys and girls looking wonderingly up at him, he would allow a smile to come over his face. 'Listen, young ladies and gentlemen' (for some reason he never called us boys and girls), 'listen, really listen! You are greater than you think you are! You can, if you believe, really believe, that you can. And,' he added, 'that is the one important thing I want to teach you in this class.'

One reason we can achieve is that built into every one of us is something I have been calling the Plus Factor. And this power or energy, this motivational quotient, can lift us out of the ordinary and above the mediocre. It is the Plus Factor that helps a person handle all the problems of life. This Plus Factor can make achievers of you and of me and of everyone who lets it take over.

The Plus Factor is closely allied to the mental attitude which I have called positive thinking. And just what is positive thinking? Well, naturally, it is the opposite of negative thinking. It is the 'I can' principle as contrasted with the 'I can't' way of thinking. It is believing in your possibilities and disbelieving in your doubts.

Positive thinking is not just a matter of 'thinking big.' It may express itself in small ways, but these add up to something big. For example, you may awaken in the morning and your first thought is, *This is going to be a lousy day*. Your wife, already cheerily getting breakfast, asks, 'And how are you this morning, Honey?' And the negative thinker comes up with the habitual reply, 'Oh, I don't feel good. I'm just all out of energy. I'm pooped!' The trouble with such a response is that it really isn't true. He is just *thinking* 'pooped'.

Perhaps you are a salesman and on your schedule for that day is a really tough buyer. 'I can't get through to that guy. He won't buy.' So it goes, 'I don't feel good.' And 'I can't.' Two self-defeating negatives. So the negative thinker goes his uninspired way throughout the day, thinking and talking himself down—the victim of the three pernicious 'L's'—lack, loss, and limitation.

By and large, there are two basic types of thinking. One is negative thinking; the other is positive thinking. And negative thinking is a very hazardous procedure, because it blocks the flow of the Plus Factor.

There is a law called the law of attraction—like attracts like. Birds of a feather flock together. Similarly, thoughts of a kind have a natural affinity. If habitually we send out negative thoughts into the world around us, into our personal world, into our business world, we tend to draw back negative results to ourselves. Thoughts spoken, or even unspoken, possess strong vibratory power. They set forces in action which, inevitably, produce outcomes precisely as conceived, articulated, and affirmed. It is a law of mind that negative thinking, negative attitudes, negative mental pictures are bound to result in negative outcomes.

If you are currently experiencing negative conditions in your life or career, such a situation did not just happen, nor is it necessarily due to 'bad breaks'. It just might be the natural and inevitable result of the nurture and projection of negative mental attitudes.

This defeatism may have been germinating in your mind for a long time. Perhaps it has made a negative thinker and receiver of you.

But I have good news for you, *great* good news, and it's this—you can change and become a positive thinker with the positive good of the Plus Factor flowing into your personality, into your business, into your relationships. And I hope you realize that the time for this personal change is now. For if you don't do it now, there is a danger that you may never do it.

The positive thinker is an optimistic, faith-motivated person who habitually projects positive images and attitudes—every day sending creative and positive thoughts into the world around him. These strong thought waves condition the surrounding world positively and positive outcomes are activated. What you send out mentally over a long period of time will return to you in kind, precisely and inevitably. So, if you really want to succeed, or having become successful want to move further on, it is crucially important to change radically from destructive negative thinking to creative positive thinking.

The Creator made each one of us in His own image and breathed into us the breath of life. That means energy, enthusiasm, optimism. I can't remember ever seeing a negative baby. They seem to be positive by nature. But some are born into negative families, and since babies are sensitive to the atmosphere in which they are reared, they take on negative characteristics. Such babies grow up with low opinions of themselves, putting themselves down as natural-born failures or losers.

What you conceive
you can achieve.

He qualified as a philosopher, I thought. For what a person becomes is what he or she tattoos on the mind over a long period of time. But the fact is, it need not be 'Born to lose.' It can be 'Born to win.'

George Hallas, famous coach of the Chicago Bears, of the National Football League, had a slogan prominently displayed on his office wall, 'Always go to bed a winner.' A wise thought indeed. During sleep the thoughts of the conscious mind may permeate the subconscious. And George Hallas did not want his players to think losing thoughts. So never take defeatism to bed with you. Imagine yourself winning as you drift off to sleep, and let the image of success germinate. It will have a wonderful effect.

Once walking through the twisted little streets of Kowloon in Hong Kong, I came upon a tattoo studio. In the window were displayed samples of the tattoos available. On the chest or arms you could have tattooed an anchor or flag or mermaid or whatever. But what struck me with force were three words that could be tattooed on one's flesh, 'Born to lose'.

I entered the shop in astonishment and, pointing to those words, asked the Chinese tattoo artist, 'Does anyone really have that terrible phrase, Born to lose, tattooed on his body.'

He replied, 'Yes, sometimes.'

'But,' I said, 'I just can't believe that anyone in his right mind would do that.'

The Chinese man simply tapped his forehead and said in broken English, 'Before tattoo on body, tattoo on mind'.

Coach Hallas was on sound psychological ground too. It is a fact that there is a deep tendency in human nature to become precisely what we image ourselves as being over a long period of time. The image of ourselves that we hold in consciousness strongly tends to reproduce itself as fact. If, for example, you suffer from an inferiority complex and constantly image yourself as inadequate, in effect disbelieving in yourself, this process will ultimately make you exactly as imaged.

You can, however, get your self-image normalized and begin to think of yourself as an adequate and capable person. Do this and you will become as visualized.

This is not just theory. This is a fact, as I know from personal experience. As a young boy I had an acutely painful inferiority attitude. I was shy, timid, and bashful. That word means abashed. I shrank from going among people. I imaged myself as being very short on ability and totally lacking in any talent. I saw myself as a nobody. Then I found that people were agreeing with me. It is a fact that others will unconsciously take you at your own self-evaluation.

But new self-knowledge came one day during my second year in college in a course in economics. The professor, Ben Arneson, later became a lifelong friend. As the class session closed he said, 'Peale, stay a few minutes.' He looked searchingly at me, 'What's the matter with you? Just why are you such a worm? You go skulking around like you're scared. When I ask you a question in class you get red in the face and tongue-tied when I am sure that you know the material very well indeed. And,' he added, 'why don't you get over this inferiority complex and act like a man?'

65

Though angered by this seemingly ruthless treatment, I had to admit he was right about me. 'I don't know,' I said 'I guess I'm just a failure.'

'Don't ever say such a negative thing! Never even think it,' he thundered, 'Draw on your faith. Ask your Heavenly Father, who made you, to change you,' he said more kindly.

I stumbled out of the classroom, along the hall, and out of the building down the long flight of outside steps. On the fourth step from the bottom I stopped. And on that particular step one of the greatest things in my life happened. There I started on the road to believing in myself.

This is how it happened. I stood completely discouraged and hopeless. Then I did what I had been taught to do. I prayed! It was a simple, desperate prayer. The poet James Russell Lowell in 'The Cathedral' has a passage:

I, who have ever prayed at morning and at eve,
Thrice in my life perhaps have truly prayed.
Thrice thrust beneath my conscious self
Have felt that perfect disenthralment which is God.

Well, anyway, this time I meant the prayer with all my mind. 'Look, Lord,' I said, 'You can change a thief into an honest man or a drunk into a sober person. Why can't you change a mixed-up, defeated guy like me into a normal person? Amen.'

I guess I expected a miracle, but nothing happened right away except that I felt peaceful and sort of happy.

Subsequently, another professor started me reading Emerson and Thoreau, Marcus Aurelius, and William James, writers who taught what could happen when a person learns to think right. I learned that I could alter my life by altering my attitudes of mind. Gradually I came to have a normal belief in myself, discovering that the Plus Factor will come to our aid if we let it. I made the most important discovery of all: that we can if we think that we can.

8

The Plus Factor of Courage

One human characteristic that has been admired since the dawn of time is the ability to face danger or suffering bravely. And closely related to this ability is the capacity to make right decisions when facing difficult moral choices. We call these special qualities *courage*—and very few among us can afford to be smug or contented about our possession of it. The truth is, most of us are afraid of something, and we're never quite sure how we'd react if suddenly we were called upon to face that which we fear.

Fortunately, there is inside each of us a hidden power that can and does help us respond to such emergencies. I have been calling that power the Plus Factor, and many times I have heard or read about extraordinary happenings where this power flowed into the lives of people in dangerous or desperate circumstances, supplying them with almost incredible strength and stamina as well as the resistance to fear that we call bravery or heroism.

Consider what happened a few years ago at a Pacific Coast beach near San Francisco. It was early in May. Two freshmen at San Francisco State College, Shirley O'Neill and Albert Kogler decided to take a swim. They plunged into the rough surf with Al in the lead, swam out beyond the breakers, and floated lazily in calm deep water about fifty yards from shore. 'Sure beats sitting in the library, doesn't it?' Al said and Shirley nodded contentedly. What neither of them knew was that homing in on them out of the depths was the most terrifying and deadly of all living creatures, a great white shark.

The great white shark is the most fearsome killer in the animal kingdom. Often it reaches a length of fifteen feet, a ton or more of streamlined muscle, its great jaws with triangular razor-edged teeth capable of cutting a man in half. As it drives through the water its round black eyes seem devoid of any sort of intelligent purpose, just a blind malignancy with one fixed intent: to rend and destroy.

Shirley heard a scream as a giant gray form suddenly seemed to rise into the air and hurl itself upon Al. His head disappeared under water suddenly crimsoned with blood, then reappeared, his face contorted with agony. 'Get away, Shirley,' he shrieked. 'Get away! It's a shark!'

Shirley O'Neill felt as if her heart had stopped beating. For half a second, she could not move. *Get away,* every fibre of her being screamed, *get away!* She turned toward shore, seized with a terror beyond description. Death was there in the water with her. Death would choose her for its next victim. She was sure of it.

But then she stopped swimming for shore. Something made her stop. Something made her turn back, back into the crimson water where the shark was still thrashing, back where the water boiled and churned, now blood red. Back toward her friend she swam. She reached for his hand, and drew back in horror. His arm had been torn from his shoulder.

Surely the shark would return. Surely it would attack again. Surely this young girl had every excuse, every reason to try to save herself.

But she did not try to save herself. Instead she swam close to Al and put her arm around his chest. 'Lie still, Al. Don't try to swim. Lie still!'

On her back, stroking with her free arm, kicking with her legs, slowly she began to tow him toward the beach. Slowly, slowly, with a plume of blood trailing behind, blood that could attract other man-eaters, or the same one. Waves washed over her head. Al's body seemed to grow heavier, second by second. But he was still alive. She would not abandon him. She would not let him go.

Now they were in the breaking surf, and her feet touched bottom, but she could go no farther. She could only call feebly for help, and the roar of the surf drowned her cries. But miraculously, farther down the beach, a surf fisherman saw her. In a flash, Joe Intersonine was racing down the beach. With a perfectly aimed cast, he dropped his line close to Shirley. She wrapped it around her waist. He reeled in, dragging her and her torn, bleeding burden into shallow water.

Now people came running from all directions. One laid a blanket over Al. He was still conscious, but just barely, and Shirley O'Neill, a Catholic, who knew that Al had never accepted any form of religion, asked if she might baptize him. When he nodded his assent, she ran to the ocean, dipped up sea water in her bathing cap, knelt beside Al, drew the sign of the cross on his forehead and baptized him 'in the name of the Father, and of the Son, and of the Holy Ghost.' Then a stretcher was brought, and Al was taken to the hospital. Two hours later, he died.

So the earthly life that Shirley O'Neill was trying to save ended. But believers would say, I think, that for Albert Kogler, eternal life began. The question is, what was the power that came to a young college freshman in the face of the most terrifying of all possible threats and gave her the courage and the selflessness to act as she did?

I think it was the power that God has planted deep in all of us. I think it was the Plus Factor.

Sometimes in an unforeseen crisis like the one faced by Shirley O'Neill there has been no previous fear, no built-in dread. So perhaps the reservoir of courage has not been drained. But can the Plus Factor make its appearance where there is a long-standing, deep-rooted fear that has saturated the whole personality of a person? I think it can. Consider the case of Naomi Clinton of Camden, South Carolina.

Some people go through life with a terrible fear of fire, usually the result of some traumatic experience in childhood. Naomi Clinton was such a person. Twice in her life she had seen her family home burned to the ground. Whenever she left her own home and her children, Naomi Clinton worried about their safety. Fear of fire was never far from her mind.

Driving home from a business convention in Florida one day, Naomi Clinton saw a pillar of black smoke rising above the highway a short distance in front of

71

her. As she drew nearer she saw several cars on the side of the road and a handful of people staring in horror at a truck that had overturned and had burst into flames. Drums of oil that had fallen from the truck were scattered about. Naomi Clinton wanted to avert her eyes and drive on, but the flames were leaping higher, blocking the road. She had to stop. She could feel the familiar terror building up in her, but she got out of her car and joined the onlookers.

That was when she saw the driver of the truck, lying there in the fire like a heap of burning rubble. As Naomi Clinton watched she saw one hand rise above the flames, waving, flapping. Then, somehow, the burning man raised his head and looked through the smoke at her.

It was a sight Naomi Clinton would never forget. 'I could see his eyes. They were filled with anguish, so big and staring. And his mouth was moving. I could see the cry on his lips, so faint and weak that I could not hear it. The roar of the fire blotted it out. Everyone else was just standing there, looking.

'At that moment an uncontrollable feeling came over me. Before I thought, or let anything enter my mind, I began running toward the burning man. Somebody shouted, 'Don't be crazy. Those oil drums will explode any second!' The burning man's arm flopped down, then rose again. It seemed to say, *Help me, I'm burning!*

'My dread of fire tugged at me, telling me "No! No! No!" But a Power much greater than fear, a Power that I can't understand, took control of me. I shook off the man who was trying to hold me back and ran through the burning grass to that blackened, outstretched hand. The truck driver's clothes were on fire. He was trying to lift himself up, but he couldn't.'

Naomi Clinton weighed only 111 pounds. Somehow she got her hands under the man's armpits and started to drag him away from the blazing truck. Heat was scorching her bare arms and legs. There was fire everywhere. A tire exploded with a roar and showered her with chunks of burning rubber that bit into her neck and singed her hair. She kept dragging the man off the burning grass and onto the roadway. When she got him there, she beat at his smouldering clothes with her bare hands, then threw herself upon him trying to smother the flames with her own body.

When the police and an ambulance finally came, Naomi Clinton was in such a state of fear and shock that she could barely answer questions. When she tried to go back to her car, her legs gave way, and she sank to the ground.

The truck driver, though terribly burned, did survive. Mrs. Clinton was given a special award for heroism by the governor of South Carolina, and later received a silver Carnegie Medal.

How did she do such a thing, this tiny woman who was so petrified of fire? She was able to do it because, to use her own words, 'a Power much greater than fear took control of me.'

Naomi Clinton believed that Power came straight from God. And I think she was right, because that's where the Plus Factor comes from.

It's strange how often people who react wisely and strongly in an emergency feel that the wisdom and the strength came to them, not from an act of will or determination on their part, but from some mysterious source that they cannot identify. They are quite candid about this; usually they are the first to admit it. Such was the case with John Skerjanec, a power-line foreman for the Southern Colorado Power Company.

Skarjanec had been checking power lines in the mountains west of Red Canyon Park and was headed back to the company offices, driving a half-ton pick-up truck over the winding mountain roads. Early in the afternoon he came to U.S. 50, a two-lane macadam road, not far from the point where it begins a steep descent in a stretch called Eight Mile Hill. That was a very dangerous piece of road; five people had been killed there in the previous three years.

As Skerjanec stopped at the intersection, a car flashed past him, going downhill so fast that he knew something was wrong. Two women were in the car. One was clutching the wheel. The other was waving her arms and screaming. It was obvious that the brakes of the car had failed, and the gears had been stripped also. It was hurtling down the mountain completely out of control. Ahead of it lay at least five miles of steep grades and hairpin mountain curves.

Skerjanec swung his truck onto the road behind the runaway car and stepped on the gas. 'And it was a strange thing,' he said later. 'I was already planning exactly what I was going to do. The idea just seemed to come to me from nowhere. I don't know how I thought of it, because I had never heard of it being done before, but it seemed the only possible way I could keep those women from flying off the road.'

The runaway car was going seventy-five miles per hour. It took a mile for Skerjanec to catch up with it. He knew that just ahead was a relatively straight stretch of road perhaps a mile long. If he was to pass

74

❧

Courage isn't always physical. There is such a thing as moral courage. The kind of courage that enables you to do what you know is right, even when— especially when — it seems expedient to do something else.

❧

the car, it had to be then. He floored his accelerator; the truck shot forward; the needle on its speedometer registered eighty-five miles per hour.

Now they were roaring down the road side by side. The danger to both vehicles was enormous. If they so much as touched fenders all the occupants would be dead. But Skerjanec's mind was locked around 'the idea that came from nowhere.' He pulled in front of the runaway car watching it in his rear-view mirror. When it was directly behind him, he began to slow down, hoping that the woman driver would not panic. He waited until her front bumper touched his rear bumper. The cars bounced apart, but he knew the woman understood what he was attempting to do, and was trying to help him. The bumpers touched again, solid contact this time. Gingerly, gradually, Skerjanec began to apply his brakes. As the speed lessened, he threw his truck into second gear. Ahead loomed a sharp curve. But the combined drag of brakes and engine was enough. Just before they reached the curve, both cars shuddered to a stop.

Where did the 'know what to do' come from? And the determination? And the driving skill? And the courage? The courage that made it possible for John Skerjanec to risk his life in an attempt to save two total strangers? No doubt about it. The courage came from the same source that Naomi Clinton's courage came from. It came from the God-given gift that I call the Plus Factor.

Courage isn't always a physical thing. There is such a thing as moral courage, too. This is the kind of courage that enables an individual to do what he or she knows is right, even when—especially when—it seems expedient to do something else. Many great men

76

have displayed it—that's why they were great. Martin Luther facing his detractors at the Diet of Worms and saying, 'It is neither wise nor prudent to do aught against the dictates of conscience. Here I stand; I cannot do otherwise.' Abraham Lincoln facing the crisis of civil war. Some of his advisors thought he should not resort to force. Horace Greeley said to him, 'If you lose, you drench the country with blood; if you win, you only pin the country together with bayonets.' But Lincoln had a vision of a united land, and the moral courage to fight and to preserve it. Because he persevered, our country is what it is today.

Sometimes moral courage enters into the highly physical realm of sports. One December evening a young football coach stared through a Birmingham hotel window at the dark Alabama night outside. This was a situation he had hoped he would never have to face. He had been head coach at Georgia Tech for only seven years. In that short time he had reversed a long losing trend in Tech football. His Yellow Jackets had battled hard all season long, finally winning the chance to play favored Michigan State in the post-season All-American Bowl on New Year's Eve. Tech was the underdog, but Coach Bill Curry had a lot of confidence in his young players. At least, he had had a lot of confidence in them . . . until now.

Word had come to him that four of the key players of his team had broken training. With the all-important game just forty-eight hours away, four of the players had failed to observe the curfew deadline. After a team dinner designed to ease tensions and relax taut nerves, they were supposed to be in bed at a certain time. But a bed check by assistant coaches had revealed that the first-string quarterback, a flanker back, a split end,

77

and the reserve fullback were not where they were supposed to be—in bed.

What should the penalty be? If the coach disqualified them from playing in this crucial game, Tech would almost certainly lose. How could Tech possibly win under those conditions? If Curry suspended his players and lost, the storm of criticism would be furious. If he announced his intention of suspending them, the pressure to rescind the order would be enormous. All the acceptance and popularity that Curry had built up during the year would be on the line. The most important game Tech had played in years would be in jeopardy. And yet . . .

And yet, the players had known the rules. They had broken them. How would they ever learn the importance of self-discipline, self-control, if they were given a tap on the wrist and allowed to play? How would the players feel who *had* obeyed the rule? What was the *right* thing to do?

When he asked himself that question and when he prayed about it, Coach Curry knew the answer. He issued the orders: The offending players would not be allowed to play in the game.

Was the Plus Factor operating here? Of course it was. It is always operating when a person making a difficult decision chooses the one that is morally right. And when the Plus Factor is thus injected into a situation, remarkable things can happen.

Take that football game, for example. The back-up quarterback, Todd Rampley, was only a sophomore. The pressure on him was terrific; he might have made all sorts of mistakes. Instead, he played the game of his life. Linebacker Ted Roof, Tech's defensive captain, said, 'It's time to circle the wagons and play harder.'

Incredibly, in the closing minutes, Tech scored a touchdown that gave them a sensational 17-14 victory.

If you had been in the stadium at Legion Field in Birmingham that night, you would not have been able to see the Plus Factor, because it is always invisible. But you could have felt it, as an underdog football team, crippled by the loss of its key players, rose up with a mighty surge of courage and determination and won the game.

Courage, says my big Webster's dictionary, is 'the firmness of spirit that faces extreme danger or difficulty without flinching or retreating.' It points out that the word itself is derived from the Latin word for heart; brave hearts have the courage to endure, and I think it is often the Plus Factor that provides such courage. Let me end this chapter by telling you of an episode that happened a few years ago in the forested hills of Kentucky.

As he pushed through the thick brush that sunny day, Marshall Clouse was a happy man. He was seventy-nine years old and blind in one eye, but he carried his chain saw and woodcutting tools easily, and he was doing what he liked to do, cutting trees to be carted back to the little sawmill he had owned for the last twenty years. He had parked his pickup truck a hundred yards away, just off the old dirt road. He expected to be home by suppertime. No one knew exactly where he was.

He felled a couple of trees with no difficulty. Then, as a tall poplar toppled, it caught in the branches of another tree. Marshall Clouse cut through the trunk of a third tree, hoping it would knock the stuck tree loose. It didn't, and so he turned away—just as both trees fell suddenly with a thunderous crash, hurling him to the ground unconscious. When he awoke, his face lacerated and bleeding, both legs were pinned under one of the fallen trees, the bones smashed, the pain almost unbearable.

Probably Marshall Clouse had never heard of the Plus Factor. But all his life he had believed in a Power greater than himself, and now he called on this Power for strength and courage. Somehow, with a screwdriver that was in his overalls pocket, he dug his shattered legs out from under the tree. He tried to move them, but they were useless. When he tried to crawl on his face, his feet caught in the vines and twigs, causing him excruciating pain. The only way he could move, an inch at a time, was on his back, dragging himself along by his elbows.

Many men half the age of Marshall Clouse would have been defeated by pain and shock. They would have decided that the truck was hopelessly distant, out of reach. They might well have chosen to lie still rather than incur the agony of moving at all.

But something inside Marshall Clouse refused to give in. Inch by agonizing inch he dragged himself, on his back, over sharp stones, through the tangled underbrush, blood flowing from his forehead, shirt ripped to shreds, useless legs trailing behind him. Inch by inch, hour after hour, as the sun dropped steadily and the chill of nightfall fell across the silent forest. On and on, biting his lips to keep from screaming, until—four hours after the trees fell on him—he was alongside the truck.

He opened the door and reached up to grasp the steering wheel so that he could pull himself into the cab. The wheel was just beyond his quivering fingers. Again he tried, gasping with pain. He could not reach it. At this point a lesser man, a man unsupported by an unconquerable determination, would have given up. But the brave heart of seventy-nine-year-old Marshall Clouse did not give up. Slowly, painfully, he began to build a little mound of leaves, dirt, twigs, anything he could reach. He built the mound and he dragged himself to the top of it. Then he reached up, grasped the steering wheel, and calling on some final reserve of strength pulled himself into the cab.

Even then, he was in a terrible predicament. His legs were useless. He could not use them to touch the brakes, or the accelerator. All he could do was start the engine, put the truck in low gear, and try to guide it as it rolled slowly downhill to the main road, back to someone who could help him. And that is what he did.

Marshall Clouse spent weeks in a hospital, then months convalescing at home. Doctors told him he would never walk again. But today, being the kind of man he is, Marshall Clouse is walking again. Not very well, perhaps. But walking.

What brought a seventy-nine-year-old man through an ordeal like that? Marshall Clouse, who has been a committed Christian for over sixty years, would tell you that the Lord Jesus did it. And he would be right. But would it not be fair to say that the Lord Jesus came to his aid by liberating in his mind and in his body the Plus Factor and the extra strength within that enabled him to rise above shattering injury, massive shock, blood loss, agonizing pain, and apparently unsurmountable obstacles?

There is no doubt at all in my mind that the Plus Factor was liberated in Marshall Clouse by a Power greater than himself. And the courage and strength it gave him saved his life.

9

Strength of a Calm Mind

*P*eace of mind is important to well-being, to successful achievement and happiness. How is it attained? One of the greatest passages in the Bible says, 'Thou wilt keep him in perfect peace, whose mind is stayed on thee . . .' (Isaiah 26:3). The word *stayed* is a reference to the ropes and stays that hold a ship's mast upright, even in the worst of storms. So it means that if your mind is braced on God—the vast, immovable, unchanging, everlasting God—the anxieties and confusions and tensions that surround you will not penetrate the peace that enfolds you. You will be quiet and controlled, without strain or stress. And this is the kind of spiritual climate in which the Plus Factor is able to grow.

Crises are going to come into every human life; that's reality. But it was a great American psychiatrist who said that attitudes toward facts can be more important than facts themselves. Thomas Carlyle had this same truth in mind when he spoke of 'the calm superiority of the spirit over circumstances.' You can react to a problem or a crisis with fear and tension and panic. Or you can follow the advice of an old Chinese philosopher who said, 'Always take an emergency leisurely.' The person who masters this art—and it is an art—will know how to overcome stress and tension.

The everyday American phrase that sums up this attitude is 'easy does it'. All great athletes have this relaxed control of themselves. The late Branch Rickey, one of the greatest baseball men of America, told me once that he wouldn't hire a player, regardless of how well he could field or hit or run, unless he was 'loose as ashes.' Now there's a picturesque and vivid phrase! Can you imagine anything looser than ashes?

Well, this is just a droll little story that I like. Peace of mind, indeed the peace of God that passeth all understanding, as Saint Paul said, is something all of us can achieve if we will just let calmness enter our minds. This is the ultimate control of tension.

There is a passage in the fourth chapter of Saint Mark's Gospel that anyone who suffers from tension or anxiety should read. Those verses describe Jesus asleep in the stem of a small boat on the Sea of Galilee when a storm arose.

The Bible account vividly portrays the fear and distress of the disciples. They knew they were in a highly dangerous situation. They were blinded by rain driven horizontally into their faces. The sail may well have been torn away. Lightning was blazing, thunder was crashing all around them. They groped their way to the stern of the lurching boat where Jesus was lying asleep, head pillowed on His arm, relaxed as healthy people are in slumber. They shook Him awake, calling out in terrified voices, 'Master, save us! We're all going to die!'

He opened His eyes and looked at the storm-lashed sea, at the frightened faces around Him. I can imagine His smile as He stood up, crossed the wet planking, clasped the mast, a tall, broad-shouldered figure, hair soaked, drenched to the skin. Then He raised one arm aloft and in a voice that carried above the shrieking of the wind uttered just three words:

'Peace, be still!'

And as the writer of the Gospel says with such simplicity, 'There was a great calm.'

I have wondered sometimes where that calm was. In the actual waves of the sea? Yes, undoubtedly. But wasn't it even more significantly in the minds of the

---

❧

This is a story about a tourist who came upon an old Indian sitting half-asleep outside his adobe home. The tourist, a hard-driving banker from the East, felt a bit indignant about this; so he said to the Indian, 'Chief, why don't you go into town and get yourself a job?' The old Indian opened one eye and said, 'Why?'

The banker said, 'Because they're paying good money these days. You might make as much as two hundred dollars a week.' And the old Indian said, 'Why?'

The banker said, 'If you started earning two hundred dollars a week, you could save your money and invest it. Then you could retire and not work anymore.'

Then the old fellow opened both eyes and said, 'Not working now!'

Was the Indian lazy—or was he right?

disciples? Fear was driven out. Panic was gone. In their regained calmness of spirit the waves must not have looked so terrifying.

What a sensational example of Christ's power at work! His was a tremendous personality, so strong, so compelling that it brought calm to the raging seas and peace to the terrified minds of His companions! No wonder they whispered in awe to one another, 'What manner of man is this, that even the winds and the seas obey him?'

I think we ought to remind ourselves that Jesus rides with us in the small boats which are our lives, boats often beset by tempests and stormy seas. Let Him hold up His hand and say to us, 'Peace, be still.' And then we can say, 'And there was a great calm.'

It calms and soothes the spirit to read the Bible, to pray, to meditate on the goodness of God. It helps to affirm that the power of God resides in you and is available to you. Not long ago I found it helpful to write an affirmation along these lines that I keep in my wallet and repeat to myself now and then. It is a statement that I have found both tranquilizing and strengthening. Here it is:

I affirm that the Plus Factor, a manifestation of God's power, is rising in me,

Renewing and healing my body,

Bringing power to my mind,

Giving me success in my work.

I affirm health, energy, enthusiasm, the joy of life.

All this I owe to Jesus Christ, my Lord and Savior.

He has given me the victory principle
For which I thank Him every day.

Here is another powerful idea that can be of tremendous value to anyone who wishes the Plus Factor to operate with strength and efficiency. The Bible tells us that Jesus gave His disciples authority over evil spirits. Why, then, shouldn't we, who are also His disciples, take authority over the devils of doubt and fear and anxiety and tension that block the flow of the life force in us?

Imagine those negative forces arrayed against you like an enemy army, threatening, malevolent, poised to attack. Then, in your mind's eye, see yourself putting on your spiritual armor, drawing your sword, charging headlong into those hostile ranks, confident that God Himself is on your side.

Summon up this image, not just once, but over and over again. Gradually, if you are truly determined to establish your authority over these destructive elements, the powerful, creative forces of the Plus Factor will begin to work unhindered through your being.

Modern science is just beginning to understand the power latent in a relaxed and peaceful mind. It is also beginning to understand the importance of a relaxed body. Almost everyone, by now, is aware of the benefits of simple muscle control. It can be practiced quite easily. To achieve a state of physical relaxation, begin by getting into a comfortable position. Then you say to the muscles controlling your face, 'Let go,' and image serenity stealing across your countenance. Then you say to your lungs, 'Breathe deeply and tranquilly; let go.' Go down to the muscles of the legs, the toes;

*Attitudes towards
facts
can be more
important
than facts
themselves.*

say 'Let go.' Stretch out your hand slowly, palm upward; then turn it over and say, 'I am now pouring all my troubles, all my tensions, all my anxieties into the great, all-powerful hand of God.' *Let them all go.*

Muscle tensions can tie us into knots; but muscle tensions are created and controlled by thoughts. When you can get your mind into harmony with God's power, it can direct the muscles of your body to relax and function smoothly.

Of vast importance in achieving peace of mind is dealing with the contents of the mind itself: the mass of ill thoughts you have stored up over the years, all the regrets, all the futilities, all the hidden sins, all the hates, all the grudges, all the vindictiveness. The minds of many people are filled with pockets of poison. And the poison flows out from these pockets through the whole personality, making fingers tremble, causing the heart to beat more rapidly and the blood pressure to rise, increasing stress and tension.

When your mind is thus filled (dogged might be a better word), you are everlastingly living at too high a tempo because of a deep, subconscious feeling that you should be punished. You are trying to get away from this feeling. But there can be no peace in your mind until you empty your mind by confession and by the cleansing that can come only from God. This is the most healthful experience that can come to anyone.

Not long ago I was preparing to retire in my hotel room in a city where I had just made a speech. The phone rang. A woman's voice said, 'If I send a car for you, will you come out and see my husband? Nobody seems able to cure him.'

I said, 'Madam, I am not a doctor.'

88

'I know that,' she said. 'But all the doctors say that his illness is the kind that only a spiritual treatment can cure.'

'I'm sorry,' I said, 'but I'm no faith healer. I believe that faith can heal, but if you expect me to heal your husband, I don't want you to be disillusioned.'

'My husband has great faith in you,' she said.

'Faith in me won't get him anywhere,' I said. 'Has he any faith in God?'

'He hasn't gone to church very often,' she confessed. 'I guess he's been too busy making money. Please come. We both need you.'

The car came for me. It took me to a large, impressive house, almost a mansion. The man was a big, burly fellow, a hard-driving, self-made type. 'What is your trouble?' I asked him.

'I'm nervous,' he said. 'I can't sleep. I have funny feelings in my arms. This one is so stiff I can't raise it properly.' And he demonstrated. 'The doctors don't seem to know anything. They tell me that physically my arm is all right. They say my trouble is my mental attitude.'

Then we sat down and talked. 'How is business?' I asked him.

'Oh, it's all right,' he said. 'But exasperating things keep happening. Recently I brought a young fellow into the firm and he double-crossed me!'

'How did he do that?' I asked.

He told me at length, ending, 'I got rid of him. He still thinks I owe him money. But he will never get it out of me.'

'I take it you don't like him much,' I suggested.

89

'I used to like him,' he said, 'but not now. No more. I hate him. I'd give my right arm to beat him up.'

His wife, who was sitting by, said, 'That is the trouble. My husband is filled with ill will and hate.'

I asked her to leave us alone for a while. When she had gone, I said to the man, 'Tell me, have you committed sin? Better get it out. It festers. Perhaps this is connected with how you feel.'

He hesitated for a while. Then he said, 'Yes, I have done some things I regret. It's strange; I never did want to be a bad person. Some of the things I've done—I would give my right arm if I had never done them.' He really meant it. That he would give his right arm, curiously, the arm he couldn't raise, was recurrent in his speech.

'Listen,' I said to him. 'I'm no healer. But I am going to put my hand on your shoulder. I probably should put it on your head, because I believe that's where the trouble really is. But I am going to put my hand on your right shoulder. You are filled with all kinds of poison and you must pour it out.'

I was there for a long time listening to him.

When he got through he looked up at me and asked, rather pathetically I thought, 'Did you ever hear anything worse?'

'Yes,' I answered, 'but you are now being cleansed, for you have emptied out your mind. Now ask your Savior for mercy.' He did that most appealingly. I prayed, 'Come into this man's troubled mind and give him peace.'

A few months later I met him again. I hardly knew it was the same man. 'Look at this arm,' he said, raising it easily above his head. 'The pain in my shoulder is gone. My head is all right, too. I have learned to follow Jesus Christ, and He has given me peace as you said He would.'

Confession. Repentance. It's as simple as that. Empty out all the pockets of poison in your mind, every one of them, and let Jesus Christ fill your mind with His healing power. That is the secret of having mental peace. That is the way to activate the flow of the Plus Factor.

10

Turn Hope to Reality

*H*ave you ever stopped to wonder what it is that keeps you going from one day to another? What lies behind your ability to fight your way through periods of discouragement or depression? What makes you believe that sooner or later bad times will get better?

It's a little four-letter word that has enormous power in it. Power to bring failures back to success. Power to bring the sick back to health. Power to bring the weak back to strength. It's the word called *hope*.

Saint Paul knew how powerful hope is. He put it right up alongside faith and love as the three great words with power in them.

Most of the memorable people I've known have been strong hopers. Sometimes they had to *learn* to hope; they had to walk before they could run. I had a friend, R. P. Ettinger, who was founder of the publishing house of Prentice-Hall, Inc. He was brilliant, articulate, and forceful, an outstanding businessman.

I first got to know him because his firm published my books, and we became warm friends.

Then R. P. Ettinger developed cancer of the throat. It was necessary to remove his larynx, and this man whose voice had dominated so many business conferences became speechless. One day in my office I had a telephone call from his wife. She said, 'You know Dick can't speak now. But he's written me a note, and it says, 'Get Norman on the telephone and ask him to speak a word of hope to me."' She said, 'You'll hear no answer, because he can't say anything, but he will be hearing you, whatever you choose to say to him.'

Right there, with no warning, I had to give this afflicted man a word of hope. I said, 'R. P., you and I published *The Power of Positive Thinking* and we are believers.' Then I gave him that familiar passage from the book of Psalms: Why art thou Cast down, O my soul? and why art thou disquieted within me? hope thou in God: for I shall yet praise him, who is the health of my countenance, and my God' (Psalms 42:11). 'Just keep on believing and hoping and thinking positively,' I said.

His wife came back on the phone. 'Say that again for him,' she said. 'He wants to copy it down. Repeat it slowly, please.'

So once again I said, 'Dick, this is the word of hope that you wanted. I'll repeat it again, and you write it down, and read it and believe it and hang onto it.' And slowly I repeated Psalms 42:11.

That little seed of hope took root, and it grew. He began to hope that he would speak again, and thanks to medical science and a mighty effort on his part the day came when he *did* speak again, and he presided once more over business conferences with assurance and power. When people asked him how he did it, he always smiled and said, 'Hope turned me around.' Or sometimes he would say quite simply, 'I was saved by hope.'

If you look back through history you will see many shining instances where a single man or woman brought hope and courage and endurance to a whole nation: Winston Churchill in the Battle of Britain; George Washington at Valley Forge; Joan of Arc, that extraordinary peasant girl, calling out to the soul of France. The Plus Factor was surging through the lives of such people, energizing them, sustaining them, filling them with unconquerable hope.

There's something about hope that makes clear thinking possible. When you're faced with a problem, do you regard it with hope or with despondency? If you hope there is a solution, if you believe that somewhere there's a solution, you are probably going to find it. If you think dismally about it, you're likely to come up with dismal results.

I know a remarkable woman who demonstrates the tremendous power of hopeful thinking. She is living proof that such thinking keeps the mind clear to function at maximum efficiency. At a meeting of the directors of a business organization where she is an executive, a really tough problem was under discussion. They wrestled with it for quite a while. The five men present came to the gloomy conclusion that there was just no solution.

But not this woman. 'Look,' she said, 'what is a problem? Simply a set of circumstances for which there seems to be no solution. But actually there is always a solution. All we have to do is find it. Then there will be no more problem.' The men around the table grinned sadly at what they considered a totally naive remark.

'Now,' she continued, 'the first step is to start thinking hopefully. Let's get rid of all this dismal thinking, because it's paralyzing us. Let's affirm that there is a solution, and that we're smart enough to find it.' This cleared the air, and the minds around that conference table began to do some real thinking. They reviewed the matter step-by-step, found the error, and without too much trouble corrected it. All because one positive person injected hope into what seemed like a hopeless situation.

We should never write off anything as impossible or as a failure. God gave us the capacity to think our way through any problem. The hopeful thinker projects hope and faith into the darkest situation and lights it up. As long as the thought of defeat is kept out of a person's mind, victory is certain to come sooner or later.

Is there a difference between hoping and wishing? Yes, there is. Hope has the quality of expectancy in it. When you hope strongly, something in you *expects* to have that hope realized. And this intangible called expectancy, which is closely allied to the Plus Factor, can affect events in a remarkable way.

All parents know that if you expect your children to live up to certain standards, and let them know that this is what you expect, they are likely to measure up. Football coaches know that if they expect a player to do well, usually he will. On the other hand, if they expect or predict poor performance, they are likely to get it.

Psychologists have labeled this phenomenon, 'The Theory of the Self-fulfilling Prophecy.' Some interesting experiments have been carried out by Dr. Robert Rosenthal, a Harvard University psychologist, to prove the truth of this theory. This professor went into a ghetto area of San Francisco where school children were undisciplined, nonachievers, poor students. He picked at random twenty-four students and divided them into two groups. He put half of these children in the hands of certain teachers, telling them that these children had tremendous potential. He assigned the other twelve children to another group of teachers, telling these teachers that the children lacked any real potential, that doubtless it would be impossible to accomplish anything with them. Then he prescribed a series of training exercises for all these students to be put through.

Six months later he returned to check on results. The students in the charge of teachers who had been told to expect good things were doing spectacular work, while the other children were, if anything, more listless and desultory than before.

What people think you expect of them, they will usually deliver. And what your own psyche, your own unconscious mind thinks you expect of it, it will deliver. When you hope strongly enough, expectancy goes to work for you. And when expectancy turns the key that we call the Plus Factor, great things happen.

You can tell strong hopers by the way they seem to be facing problems. Psychologically speaking, hopers look forward. Regretters look back. The eminent psychiatrist Dr. Smiley Blanton, who was a good friend of mine, kept in his office a tape recording of typical problems brought to him by people struggling with frustrations or disappointments. Their identities were concealed, of course, but sometimes the doctor would play the tape for a new patient and ask him or her to listen for a significant phrase that occurred over and over again. That phrase was, 'If only . . .' The unhappy people kept repeating it as they reviewed their failures, their broken relationships, their deep unhappiness. 'If only' they had made wiser decisions. 'If only' they had done things differently. On and on. If only . . . If only . . .

'You see,' Dr. Blanton would say, 'those people are bogged down in the swamp of regret. They'll never be happy until they change the direction in which they're looking. The phrase they should be repeating over and over again is not 'If only.' The phrase should be 'Next time.' 'Next time' I'll avoid all those mistakes and errors and come out with a success instead of a failure.'

Now what was Dr. Blanton saying? In one word, he was counseling *hope*. That was his prescription for dazed or despairing minds. 'Next time . . .'—that phrase is packed with hope. It lets the Plus Factor begin to stir in persons from which it has been excluded by pessimism, fear, gloom, despair.

Some years ago I spent a few days in Jamaica. At the hotel where we were staying, an old map hung in one of the hallways. Looking at it, I noticed some very faint lettering that ran across an almost uninhabited part of the island. I had to look close to make out the words, but finally I did. They said: 'The Land of Look-Behind.'

Intrigued, I asked the owner of the hotel what those words meant. He told me that in the days of slavery, runaways from the sugar plantations sometimes escaped into that lonely and barren territory. They were often pursued by slave owners or other authorities with guns and dogs. The fugitives were always on the run, always looking over their shoulders. So that was where the term came from: The Land of Look-Behind.

I never forgot that melancholy term, because my years of counseling people have led me to believe that many of them are living in their own private land of look-behind. They are the ones who dwell endlessly on past mistakes, who let fears generated by old failure rob them of success, who refuse to accept God's promises of forgiveness of sins. When a person lives in the land of look-behind, he or she is really excluding hope from his or her life. They are also making it almost impossible for the Plus Factor to operate. How can the Plus Factor make an entry into a mind that has lost the buoyancy of hope?

Speaking of buoyancy, I remember an old lithograph that a businessman friend of mine keeps in a prominent place in his office. It's not a colorful or handsome print. It shows an old, clumsy-looking scow, about three times the size of an ordinary rowboat, with high sides. From the oar locks, two oars are resting dejectedly on the sand. The tide is out and the old scow is stranded high on the beach; at the side of the picture is a glimpse of the distant water. The whole effect is rather somber; there's nothing more hopeless looking, more inert, than a beached boat. You can't pull it or drag it; it's too heavy. It's just stuck there on the sand with the water far out.

But down at the bottom of the picture is this caption: 'The tide always comes back.' And when the tide does come back, that inert thing comes alive. It rises on the mighty shoulders of the sea. It dances on the waves. The tide always comes back! I asked the owner, 'Why do you have that picture on your wall?'

✴

Hope has
expectancy in it.
When expectancy
goes to work —
great things happen
to you.

✴

He told me that he had seen it in an old antique store at a time when things were going very badly. He had bought it for a few dollars because he was very discouraged, and the message in the caption gave him a lift. It sent a flicker of hope through him every time he looked at it. That was why he kept it: to remind himself that troubles do pass, that storms do blow over, that the tide doesn't go out and stay out forever. Sooner or later it comes back in.

I've gone through some difficult times—who hasn't?—and I know how easy it is to think that troubles have become your constant companions. You let a gray film of hopelessness creep into your mind, where it colors everything. You can even begin to enjoy this sense of hopelessness, in a perverse sort of way. It gives you an excuse for not trying to improve the situation!

The remedy for this state of mind is a good strong dose of hope, given to yourself at least three times a day. Don't ever say to yourself, 'I've had it. I'm finished. I can't cope with all this.' Never think, 'This is more than I can take; it's more than I can handle.' Say aloud and affirm to yourself, 'The tide may be out just now, but it is turning and soon it will come back in!'

I remember being taught a lesson in hopefulness very early in life. When we were children, my brother Bob and I used to go every summer to visit our grandparents, who lived in Lynchburg, Ohio. Beside the house, quite close to it, was a great tree. One night, just after our grandmother had put us to bed, a tremendous storm came up. The wind whistled around the house with a sound like a thousand banshees. Lightning flashed and thunder roared. Rain was hurled in sheets against the windows. The whole house shook.

Bob and I were scared. From where I lay, I could see the tree, silhouetted against the lightning flashes. Seeing how violently it was being tossed by the storm, I was suddenly filled with terror. 'Bob,' I cried, 'the tree is falling! The tree is falling!' We jumped out of bed and scurried down to where my grandmother was sitting by a kerosene lamp, quietly reading the *Christian Advocate*. We cried, 'Grandma! Grandma!'

'What's the matter?' she asked calmly.

'The tree! It's going to fall down on us!'

My grandmother was a very wise woman. She bundled us up and took us out on the porch in the wind and the rain. She said, 'Isn't it great to feel the rain on your face? Isn't it marvelous to be out here in the wind? God is in this rain. God is in this wind. You don't have to worry about the tree. The tree is having a good time with this storm. See how it yields to it, bending one way or the other. It doesn't fight it. It cooperates with it. It's playing with the storm. It's laughing with the wind and the rain. It's not going to fall tonight. It's going to be there for a long time to come. Now, you go back to bed, boys. God is in the storm, and ultimately all storms pass.'

All through my life the memory of that simple incident has reassured and sustained me. I thought of it again not long ago when I was seated in an airliner in Washington, D.C., waiting to take off for New York. We had taxied out to the runway, when the sky became dark and sinister. A high wind came roaring up the Potomac, and sheets of rain pelted the aircraft. The plane actually rocked violently from the force of the wind. We passengers were getting very apprehensive when the voice of the pilot came on the loudspeaker. He had a soft southern accent. 'Ladies and gentlemen,' he drawled, 'there's a storm center directly above the airport. We can't take off in this weather. We're going to wait it out. Our report is that the storm will pass in about forty-five minutes. So you people who have business engagements in New York, stop fretting and sit back and relax, because we're not going to New York for a while. Meanwhile,' he went on, 'I'm going to head the plane into the wind so that you'll be more comfortable. Don't worry about anything.' And then he added these words: 'All storms ultimately pass.'

Of course they do. Believing that fact, accepting that fact, is the beginning of wisdom, the beginning of hope.

If your belief in hope includes the conviction that God is for you and will help you through any emergency, enormous power is available to you. You may never know that power is there until you need it and call upon it in some dire situation perhaps even a life-threatening situation; then you find out. I remember we published many years ago in *Guideposts* magazine, a true story where this power that I'm writing about— the power of hope backed by faith—comes through so vividly that I've never forgotten it.

Lucinda and Charles Sears lived on the edge of Lake Okeechobee in Florida. They will never forget— no one who was in southern Florida at the time will ever forget—that day in September when almost without warning one of the greatest hurricanes in history boiled up out of the Caribbean. The monstrous storm slashed into Miami, then surged up the peninsula, leaving death and destruction behind.

Lucinda Sears stood at the door of her little house with a troubled look in her eyes. She and her husband knew nothing about the full extent of the storm; this was in the days before there were hurricane warnings. All they knew was that suddenly the nine-foot earthen dike around the lake burst and water began to surge around their cabin. Moments later the roof blew off their small home as if it were a piece of cardboard. They knew they were looking into the blank eyes of death.

They grabbed their three children under their arms and ran outside looking for shelter. All they could see was one bent old tree that had withstood many a storm in the past. Whether it could withstand this one they didn't know, but it was the only hope they had. The rising water from the lake drenched them as they ran to the tree. It made everything so slippery that one of the little boys dropped from his father's arms and disappeared for a moment. Balancing the other boy with one arm, Charles finally pulled the child from the swirling muck. Floating branches and other debris battered the family as they finally made it to the tree and climbed into the sheltering branches.

The fury of the storm grew worse. As the water level rose, the terrified family climbed higher into the tree, until they were clinging desperately to the topmost branches. Water continued to rise until it came to the parents' shoulders. They could climb no higher. They had to hold the children up above their heads. It was the only way to keep them from being drowned.

As the winds lashed them and the rain stung their faces, night came on. Still the water inched relentlessly higher. 'Cindy, we're all going to die!' cried Charles.

'Be quiet,' Lucinda commanded him. 'We're not going to die. The Lord is here with us. You just hold up those children.' And the storm continued to rage. Once Charles slipped, and he and the two boys were nearly swept away. Lucinda made their little daughter, Effie Ann, lock her arms around her mother's neck. Then, with her legs wrapped around a branch, Lucinda reached down and pulled the boys up with her. She held all three children until Charles could get hold of the tree and help her again.

But still the waters reached for them in the blackness with the muddy hands of death. 'It's no use,' Charles sobbed. 'We can't hold on. We'll never make it.'

Into the storm Lucinda's strong voice cried. 'We will make it!' And then, incredibly, she began to sing, with hope in her heart, above the shrieking of the wind:

Father, I stretch my hand to Thee,
   No other help I know.
If Thou withdraw Thyself from me,
   Ah, whither shall I go . . .
Author of faith, I lift to Thee
   My weary, longing eyes;
O may I now receive that gift;
   My soul, without it, dies.

As the old hymn was borne away by the wind, Lucinda saw three flashes of light streak across the eastern sky. Perhaps it was only lightning, but to Lucinda it was a sign. 'Thank You, God. Dear Jesus, thank You,' she murmured. And the wind slackened and the night became quiet.

Slowly the water receded until at noon the next day they were able to get down from the tree, battered, hurt, hungry, exhausted, but still alive. They made their way painfully to an aid station where they found food and shelter. Thanks to the hope and faith in one woman's heart, they had lived through the terror of the night.

We have a marvelous faith by which we triumph over danger, over discouragement, over despair, over everything—a faith of no defeat.

So build hope into your philosophy. Base your life upon it. *Hope* that difficulties will pass. Hope that storms will cease. *Hope* that pain will not endure. Hope that weakness will be overcome. *Hope* thou in God . . . and ultimately you will find yourself saying, 'Praise God, from whom all blessings flow.'

11

The Thirteenth Stone

*I*n the ancient city of Kyoto, Japan, there is a famous garden that consists of nothing but thirteen large stones placed in what seems to be a random pattern on a base of carefully raked white sand.

For centuries these stones have intrigued visitors. What do they symbolize in their stark simplicity? One observer may see them as representing thirteen basic problems of mankind, each a unity in itself but also part of a greater whole. Another onlooker may decide that the stones are emblematic of thirteen different forms of happiness, and find himself wondering what those happinesses may be. Yet another observer may become aware that the stones are carefully positioned so that it is impossible to view all of them at once.

One visitor may find that the garden conveys a deep sense of peace and tranquility. Another may find his mind stimulated and somehow expanded. In a way, the garden is like the famous Rorschach inkblot tests used by psychologists and psychiatrists to gain insight into a patient's thought processes. The inkblots have no intrinsic meaning of their own, but what the viewer thinks he sees in them may give a clue to his mental or emotional condition.

The last time I was at the garden in Kyoto the concept of the Plus Factor was very much in my mind, and I began to wonder if perhaps in some way the stone garden might be a reflection of that concept. Suppose, I said to myself, the white sand symbolizes the universal nature of the Plus Factor, the truth that it is built into all of us.

And suppose further, I went on, that these thirteen stones represent attitudes or states of mind that release the Plus Factor, translating it from the general to the actual, concrete, specific needs of individual human beings?

So, choosing one stone and fixing my eyes upon it, I said to myself, 'That represents faith.' And of the next, 'That's a symbol for love.' And then, 'That's the quality of persistence.' And then, 'That one stands for the power of prayer.' I went all around the garden, assigning to each stone some positive characteristic of this kind.

The first twelve choices were quite easy, but somehow I got stuck on the thirteenth. Try as I might, I could not think of a suitable identity to bestow upon this thirteenth stone. I wrestled with it for a while and then turned away impatiently. 'What does it matter if you can't think of an appropriate name for a rock?' I said to myself. 'Who cares?' And like an echo a phrase jumped into my mind. 'Caring. Perhaps that's what it represents. The power of caring.'

Well, regardless of what that stone may or may not represent, there is no doubt whatsoever in my mind that people who care about other people, and show that caring in loving, unselfish ways, almost invariably have a strong, deep current of the Plus Factor operating within themselves. When we say of someone, 'He (or she) is a very kind person,' what we are really describing is a person who has discovered a key that unlocks the door to real happiness. And the name of that key is caring, or kindness.

The caring has to come from the heart, though. Helping people in some casual fashion, or because you have some ulterior motive for helping them, won't activate the Plus Factor. Remember how the Good Samaritan in the Bible cared about the man attacked by robbers? The Good Samaritan had nothing to gain from helping the victim, but he helped him anyway. It was the caring principle in action. And I'm sure the Plus Factor in the Samaritan's life was strengthened because of it.

Caring is an extraordinary characteristic, when you stop to think about it. Self-preservation is said to be the first law of existence. But it really isn't; there are times when the power of caring is so strong that the instinct to save one's own life at any cost is simply swept aside.

The other night on television I watched a drama based on the dreadful crash of an airliner in Washington a few years ago, a crash in which seventy-eight persons lost their lives. You may remember that the plane tried to take off in a snowstorm after waiting on the runway for a period of time that allowed ice to form on its wings. It hit one of the twin spans of the 14th Street Bridge with its tail section and crashed through the ice into the freezing waters of the Potomac River. Only a handful of dazed survivors managed to struggle to the surface. The rest went down under the black water with the plane itself.

Rescue efforts were hindered by the appalling weather and by late afternoon traffic that clogged the bridge. A rescue helicopter manned by two skilled and heroic specialists, Gene Windsor, a paramedic, and Don Usher, a pilot with many hours of Vietnam experience, flew through the whirling snow and hovered above six victims who were clinging to ice floes or the wreckage of the tail section that was still above the water. They dropped a rope right into the arms of a middle-aged man with a bald head and moustache. Instead of tying it around himself, he passed it to a woman near him. The chopper lifted her to safety.

Then it flew back and dropped the rope again. Again the bald-headed man passed it to his companions. The helicopter dragged four of them toward shore, but one woman slipped back into the icy water, too weak to hold on. As she thrashed about, a man in the crowd on the shore stripped off his coat and plunged into the freezing river. He was Lenny Skutnik, a clerk in the government's Budget Department. He said later that he had had no training in lifesaving or rescue work. But something in him cared so much that he was willing to risk his life to save the woman. And he did save her.

Meantime the chopper headed back for the bald-headed man, but he was gone. Gene Windsor said, 'I'll never forget his pale, upturned face as he watched us moving away with the others, knowing that probably he would not be there when we got back.' Twice this man, believed to have been Arland D. Williams, Jr., a bank executive from Atlanta, had handed the gift of life to a stranger at the cost of his own. Jesus had a word for such a person. 'Greater love hath no man than this, that a man lay down his life for his friends' (John 15:13).

When Gene Windsor finally called his wife to assure her that he had survived the dangers of the rescue mission and tried to tell her about the man in the water, he broke down and cried.

What is this marvelous intensity of caring that moves us so when we hear about it or witness it in action? Sometimes it appears in flashes of almost incredible heroism, as on that tragic afternoon in Washington. Sometimes it infuses a whole lifetime, as with a Florence Nightingale, or an Albert Schweitzer, who gave up a brilliant career in music to spend his days in the jungles of Africa, bringing the healing gifts of medicine to the primitive people he found living there.

There is a Christ-like quality about such people. I think it was Tolstoy who said of Lincoln that he was a 'Christ in miniature.' And so he was.

The capacity for caring doesn't always take such dramatic form; it can show through in countless little demonstrations of kindness or concern. The other day I had one of those experiences painfully familiar to air travelers. I arrived at my destination in a midwestern city, but my suitcase didn't. I waited and waited by the carousel as a procession of bags went past, but mine was not among them. I was still waiting when the captain of our flight came through the baggage area. I had exchanged a few words with him during the flight. Now he stopped and asked me if I was having a problem.

When I explained the difficulty, he nodded understandingly. 'You made a close connection in Chicago,' he said. 'Your bag will probably come in on the next flight. But don't worry about it. You go on to your hotel, and I'll see that the bag gets to you as soon as possible.'

I protested that I didn't want him to be inconvenienced, but he insisted, so finally I gave in and took a cab to my hotel. I thought the airline would send the bag along by messenger when it arrived. About two hours later there was a knock on the door. When I opened it, there stood the captain himself, gold stripes gleaming, holding my bag. It was amazing that a man in his position would go to so much trouble for a stranger, and I told him so, with profuse thanks. All he said, with a smile, was, 'Well, I knew you'd need your toothbrush!'

Caring, that's what he was, a caring person with the imagination and self-discipline to set aside his own convenience in order to help someone else. No wonder he had risen to be the captain of a great airplane. It wouldn't surprise me if some day he becomes chief executive of the whole airline, because the Plus Factor is pushing him upward.

Sometimes the Plus Factor will give an individual the insight and imagination to be helpful and caring in subtle and surprising ways. I once knew a man whose body was painfully twisted and deformed by polio. But his spirit was unconquerable. 'My body may be handicapped,' he would say, 'but my mind isn't.'

One day I asked him where this marvelous attitude came from; had he always had it? 'No,' he said, 'not always. As a teenager I was terribly self-conscious and unhappy. I never wanted to undress in a locker room or in a place where other boys could see how I looked. Even the prospect of a routine physical exam left me filled with self-loathing and dread.

111

'One day I had to endure yet another physical exam by a doctor I had never met before. He was completely impersonal and professional, but I was miserable. Afterward he told me to get dressed. Then he sat at his desk and asked me various questions, making notes on some kind of medical form that lay before him. Finally he stood up and asked me to excuse him briefly. He would be back in about ten minutes, he said. Then he left the room.

I sat there staring at the form on his desk, wondering what sort of grim notations he might have made about me. At last, unable to contain my curiosity, I went over and looked at it. There were some medical references that meant little to me, but then my eye fell on what he had written in the box reserved for "Comments." There he had written five words in a strong, clear hand: *Has a magnificently shaped head.*

'I'll never forget the extraordinary sense of gratitude and relief that flooded me when I read those words. They made me feel that I was not just a cripple, not just a freak; I was a person with compensating features and attributes. Right then and there I made up my mind to look on the bright side of things, to put my handicap in its place, to move forward and make the most of myself regardless of circumstances, regardless of anything.

'And the most marvelous component of that tremendous feeling of warmth and optimism was the knowledge that this doctor, this perceptive, caring man, had staged the whole thing. He had left the room knowing that I would be unable to resist the temptation to look at the piece of paper on his desk. He had written a prescription designed to restore my damaged ego, my shattered self-esteem. What a wonderful thing!

What a wonderful happening! It turned me completely around. It has illuminated my whole life!'

Yes, when it works through people like that doctor, the Plus Factor is a wonderful thing indeed.

Becoming a compassionate person isn't easy; sometimes a person has to go through pain and suffering before he achieves it. Certainly that was the difficult road that Detective Richard Pastorella of the New York City police force had to follow.

On the night of New Year's Eve, 1982, Detective Pastorella and his partner, Tony Senft, answered an emergency call to the plaza of a federal building in downtown Manhattan, where a bomb planted by a terrorist or a madman had gone off. No one had been injured in that explosion, but soon word was flashed that another bomb had exploded at police headquarters a few blocks away. There a patrolman, badly wounded, gasped to Detective Pastorella that he thought the bomb had been concealed in a paper bag.

Knowing that if two bombs had exploded there could easily be more, Pastorella and Senft began a search of the ground-level area of the police station with Hard Hat, a German shepherd trained to work for the bomb squad pacing alertly beside them. Suddenly, tugging at his leash, the big dog drew the officers to a darkened area near a pair of uprights that supported the building. There in the gloom Detective Pastorella saw, not one, but two paper bags. Each was placed behind one of the support columns.

And at that moment, Hard Hat sat down.

When Hard Hat sat down, Detective Pastorella knew that he and his partner were facing a situation of enormous danger. Curious bystanders were beginning to collect at the scene. He had a uniformed patrolman move them, and move Hard Hat, behind a wall some distance away. Then, with his partner behind him, he inched toward the paper bag over which he had placed a protective device known as a bomb blanket. Slowly he reached out his right hand . . . and the universe seemed to explode in his face.

The blast left him unconscious until the next day. Then he awoke to agonizing pain. His face and right arm were badly burned. There were no fingers on his right hand. One eye had been removed; he was blind in the other. Most of his hearing was gone. His partner's injuries were almost as bad.

His career as a police officer was over. For a year he was in and out of hospitals, fighting against a sense of total despair. What about his wife, Mary? What about their two teenage children? What did the future hold? There were no clear answers to such questions.

For a while fellow police officers came to see him, but eventually their visits stopped, and Detective Pastorella knew why. His plight reminded them all too vividly of the dangers they themselves faced every day.

Sometimes, I think, the Plus Factor uses other people to impart its mysterious design to us. One night after Richard Pastorella's sense of loneliness and frustration found vent in a torrent of bitter words, his wife, Mary, said to him gently, 'You're not the only one, you know. There are other cops who have been hurt, too. You're not unique.'

All night long those words seemed to dance in Pastorella's mind. The next day he wrote to police headquarters asking for a list of police officers severely injured in the line of duty. Headquarters not only sent such a list, a place was offered where Pastorella and others on the list could meet.

From that beginning came 'The Police Self-Support Group,' dedicated to helping injured policemen and their families. Now Richard Pastorella works six or seven days a week helping wives with disabled husbands, easing family tensions and quarrels, improving the psychological climate in which the children of such victims must live, helping with specific financial or medical problems, providing transportation, offering a steady source of comfort and support.

Indomitable . . . that's the word that comes to mind when I think of Richard Pastorella. It means undaunted . . . unconquered . . . unembittered. It means a life glorified by . . . the Plus Factor.

Helping someone in trouble, caring about people you hardly know, is almost a form of prayer, when you stop to think about it. It's an offering to God and the benefits flow right back to you.

Years ago I had two friends in Chicago, Gus and Frank Bering, who owned the Sherman House, a fine hotel. I remember Gus telling me about a barbers' supply convention they had in the hotel. Barbers' supply people from all over the United States were there, and some of them decided to stage a dramatic demonstration of the barber's art.

They went down to Halted Street where derelicts used to gather and they picked out the dirtiest, seediest, most disreputable-looking one they could find. They brought him back to the Sherman House and took off his ragged clothes and gave him a bath. They shaved him, they groomed his hair, they squirted after-shave lotion on him. They bought him a new suit, new shoes, the best shirt they could find, an elegant tie. They even bought him a cane and a fancy vest and an expensive hat. He looked terrific. They presented him as an example of what barbers could do for a man, and he maintained a dignified appearance throughout the convention.

Gus Bering became interested in this man, and when the convention ended he offered him a job in the hotel. He told him to report the next morning. But the man didn't show up. He didn't appear for several mornings, so Bering went down to Halsted Street to look for him. He finally found him under some newspapers in an alley, his fine clothes all torn and dirty, his face covered with stubble, his eyes bleary from drink.

Bering picked him up and put him in a taxi and took him back to the hotel and cleaned him up again. He said, 'The barbers didn't do enough for you; in fact, they didn't do anything for you; they just wanted an exhibit and you were it.'

Then, Gus Bering told me, he took the man over to the Chicago Temple, a Methodist church around the corner.

I said, 'What did you do with him over there, Gus?'

He smiled, because he knew I already knew the answer. He said, 'I got some real religion into him and he was changed. He took the job I had offered him, and he succeeded at that, and he went on to other jobs. Eventually he married and had a fine family. He turned out all right.'

What made a smart, big-time hotel owner like Gus Bering such a caring person? It was his total commitment to the greatest example of caring that this world has ever seen. I have seen countless examples

116

myself where this attitude of caring came into a person's life and changed it completely.

There is a man I have known for more than thirty years, and for many of those years he was an abject failure. You might almost say he was an expert in failure. Every job he undertook went awry. Practically everything he said was the wrong thing to say, and most of what he did was done without skill. Sometimes I would see him staring into space with so bewildered an expression that it haunted me. I tried to help him, but with no success. I knew he wasn't stupid, because from time to time his personality would display flashes of intelligence and even charm.

One night I had to drive nearly a hundred miles to give a talk, and I invited this man to come along with me, thinking we might get somewhere with his difficulties. We talked all the way there and got nowhere. He listened to my speech, but that didn't help either. On the way home he kept repeating, 'What's wrong with me? What's wrong with me?' I had no ready answer.

We stopped at a roadside restaurant for a snack. I shall never forget the beauty of that moonlit night. The entire countryside was bathed in silver radiance as we came out of the diner.

My friend was standing beside the car when suddenly he gripped my arm and shouted. 'Norman! I've got it!'

I was startled. 'You've got what?'

'I know what's wrong with me,' he said. 'I know why everything goes wrong. It's because I am wrong myself.'

I knew that he was sincere. I also knew he had taken the all-important first step in finding himself, so I asked him quietly, 'Do you know what can make you right, all the way down to the depths of your nature?'

'No,' he answered. 'I just know that I'm wrong. Can you tell me how to become right?'

So I told him, standing there in the moonlight. And he listened. For the first time, he really listened. I was reminded of this experience when I saw him the other day. He is now a leader of his community, an elder in his church; he has a wife, a lovely family, a beautiful home. But more important, and beyond all else, he is filled with the joy of living.

'Do you know what happened to me, that night we drove together?' he asked me. 'I had been breaking apart, but when I finally listened to you telling me about Jesus, suddenly I seemed to come together.'

You may say that you have observed people who have lived wrong lives and still have prospered. I, too, have observed them. But remember that God does not settle His accounts on the thirtieth of every month, or even this year, or the next, or the next. And I can tell you this: Many people I have known who insisted on living a bad life ended up badly. It isn't always a swift or dramatic occurrence. But sooner or later it comes.

Some years ago I spoke at a meeting downtown in New York sponsored by the Salvation Army. The audience was composed of several hundred of the unhappiest-looking human beings I have ever seen. Many had started out with great advantages in life, but now they were down-and-outers. To be in the presence of these wasted lives was a chilling experience, almost a frightening one.

A man came up to me afterward and told me his name. 'Why, Harry!' I said. 'What are you doing here?' I remembered him from years back, when we were both youngsters growing up in Ohio. In those days when cars were still far from numerous, he drove the sportiest one in town. He belonged to my father's church, but he didn't attend very often. He was an attractive fellow with a nice personality, but even then he drank too much and seemed concerned about no one but himself.

'What am I doing here?' he repeated. 'Well, to tell you the truth I'm here by the natural sequence of events. Cause and effect. It's probably too late, but I realize now that if people will just behave themselves, act decently and honorably, if they are just good rather than bad, abundance will come to them. If not, well . . .' he shook his head. Then he muttered, 'There are some of us who need to be saved from ourselves. I've been wrong since back in Ohio as a boy.'

'It's not too late, Harry.' Sadly he shook his head. 'There's no good in me, Norman.' But there was. The Plus Factor was there. I'm glad to say that caring eventually released it so that the rest of this man's life was good, very good.

Try caring, the compassionate kind of caring taught by Jesus. It will not only help people; it also does wonders for the person who does the caring.

12

Handling Trouble

*W*hat's the most important thing in this world for all of us? It's learning how to live, isn't it? Life is a priceless gift, but it doesn't last forever. While we have it, our happiness depends on just one thing: how well we learn to cope with the challenges it presents.

When the seas of life grow rough, when troubles come, when problems arise, the Plus Factor, that shining ingredient poured into us at birth, is ever ready to help us, sometimes in surprising ways. For example, have you ever heard of the Law of Challenge and Response? Arnold Toynbee, the great historian, believed that the key to understanding history, with its rise and fall of civilizations, lay in the action of this invisible law. He was convinced that if a civilization faced some tremendous life-threatening challenge, met it head on and survived, the energies released by that mighty effort carried that civilization to new heights of art, of literature, of every aspect of culture.

Centuries ago, when the Greeks were threatened by the overwhelming might of the Persian empire, they responded with courage and determination. They hurled the Persians back. Then they went on to astounding achievements in art, in architecture, in philosophy, in drama. Two thousand years later, the English did something very similar. They rose up to defeat the great Armada that the Spaniards sent against them. The national pride and purpose and energy thus liberated produced such literary giants as Shakespeare, the colonization of the New World, and ultimately the great British Empire on which, it was said, the sun never set.

What does all this have to do with you or me? Simply this: The same law that raised the Greeks and the English to such heights, the law that Toynbee called Challenge and Response, exists in all of us and can operate in all of us as one more manifestation of the great dormant force we have been calling the Plus Factor.

When you get right down to basics, what Toynbee was saying is that trouble can be good for you. When you look it in the eye, when you refuse to be defeated, when you make up your mind to fight back, you discover you have hidden strengths and energies that you didn't even know you had.

Now, I'm not claiming that all troubles should be welcome or that all difficulties are blessings. Some sorrows can be devastating; some troubles can be agonizing.

But you can't deal with human beings and their problems as long as I have without recognizing that a certain amount of trouble is essential for character development and spiritual growth. And this too I have

121

observed through the years: Trouble either makes a person bigger or smaller. It never leaves him exactly the way he was before. Some people break under trouble; others break records.

Sometimes the Plus Factor, called forth by this Law of Challenge and Response, appears in the form of quiet courage that faces up to bitter trials and then carries on undiminished through the years.

Not long ago, filling a speaking engagement in one of our southern states, I went into the motel dining room quite early for breakfast. It was a gray, wet morning with low hanging clouds. Outside I could see Spanish moss dripping from the trees in melancholy streamers. It was not, I thought, a day calculated to raise the spirits.

But this negative attitude was not shared by the waitress behind the counter, a cheerful black lady with a radiant smile. 'Good morning,' she said. 'Sure am glad to see this rain. Yes, sir. Bet those farmers out there are too. I can just about hear those crops agrowing on a morning like this, can't you?'

Well, I had not really been listening for crops growing, but she went right on: 'Now what can I fix you for breakfast on this fine day that the Lord has given us?'

'How about a poached egg and a little dry toast?' I asked, adding apologetically, 'I'm on a diet, you know.'

'Diet?' she said. 'Diet? Nobody ought to start a day with one little old sad-faced egg. You just sit there now and I'll bring you a real man-sized southern breakfast, eggs and sausage and biscuits and grits with red-eye gravy. Keep you going all day long!'

And despite my feeble protests, that's what she did.

122

❧

Anyone can sail
with the fair
breeze.
It is when
the seas get rough
that seamanship
really counts.

❧

It was so early that we were alone in the dining room, just the two of us.

'Tell me,' I said, 'what makes you so happy? No, don't tell me; I'll tell you. You've just got to be a Christian, a real one.'

'Yes, I surely am,' she said, and there was such a note of gladness in her voice that the whole day seemed suddenly golden, as if a shaft of sunlight had come lancing in. 'I started out mighty poorly in this life, but the Lord made me a promise and He kept it, too.'

She went on to tell me that she and her husband had been born in abject poverty. Ten years after they were married, he had been killed in a sawmill accident, leaving her with three small children, all girls. 'It was hard,' she said. 'Oh, Lord, it was so hard at times. But I had the Lord's promise, and I believed it. So I started a little dry-cleaning business and I still have it—I just come to work here in the morning because I like to meet new people and tell them about the Lord if they'll listen—and one of my girls is through college, now, and the next one is halfway through. Oh, yes, I'm a Christian, all right. It's the greatest thing anybody can be!'

'You know,' I told her, 'I've spent my whole life trying to get that message across to people. But tell me, which of the Lord's promises meant so much to you?'

'It's in the Gospel of Saint Luke,' she said. 'Ninth chapter, first verse, where it says: "Then he called his twelve disciples together, and gave them power and authority over all devils, and to cure diseases". ' She had been mopping the counter with a rag, and now she stopped and looked right into my eyes. 'You see,'

124

she said, 'there are lots of different devils. I guess every one of us has his own special devil. My devil was poverty, and that's a terrible devil because it will fill you with bitterness and hate if you let it. It will wreck your health, because you are filled with fear all the time. It will warp your mind and your soul.

'But when I remembered that Jesus said I could cast out devils in His name, and when I invited Him into my life, He drove out the fear. And when the fear was gone, do you know what happened? Well, I'll tell you. For the first time I could think. Yes, sir, my mind, free of all that hate, went to thinking. I began to think clearly. That's when I got the idea for starting my little business. And I found I could plan and have hope and move ahead without being chained down and made helpless by that devil called poverty. I cast that devil out in the name of the Lord. So when you ask me if I'm a Christian, you can see why I say I am.'

'You certainly are,' I said. 'You're a great lady. Meeting you has given me a tremendous lift. I just know this is going to be a terrific day!'

And I was so full of enthusiasm that I ate all the eggs and all the sausage and all the biscuits and even most of the grits and the red-eye gravy.

Now there was a case where the Plus Factor liberated energies that sustained and fortified a whole lifetime, and I have no doubt that it spilled over into the next generation too. And what was the trigger? Trouble was the trigger. Trouble that might have crushed or embittered some people, but in this case called forth a valid response, and the strength of mind that was equal to the challenge.

There is excitement in this concept of trouble as a dynamic force in human affairs. But you have to know how to handle it. You have to know how to respond to it. Anyone can sail with a fair breeze. It's when the seas get rough that seamanship—really understanding the sea—counts. When trouble comes in human affairs it's lifemanship—understanding the role that trouble can play in life—that makes all the difference.

There is no doubt that trouble often does burn away undesirable traits or characteristics. Take pride, for instance, or arrogance, or willfulness—these things block us from people and from our most cherished goals. Like constraining fences, they have to be broken down before we can love and be loved, before we can really join the human race. Trouble can do that.

I believe that if trouble avoids a person (or he avoids it) for too long, he may grow complacent and careless and even a bit smug. I can speak to some extent from personal experience in this. For years everything in my life went well, almost too well. People brought their troubles to me, but I had almost none of my own. Then, abruptly, I found myself at the centre of a storm of criticism. I became upset and discouraged and very unhappy. Well, I lived through that storm. But now, when people seek my help, I truly believe I'm better qualified to help them. I know how it feels, I know how it hurts, I know how vulnerable and fallible despairing humans can be. That's why I believe trouble can humanize a person. That's why I think the notion that God may use trouble for His own purposes may not be so old-fashioned or out-of-date after all.

Sometimes when I talk to people about the inevitability of trouble and the importance of it, they ask if I have any formula for dealing with it. I usually reply that since no two troubles are alike, there is no magical remedy that will deal with all of them. But then I add that there are five common-sense attitudes that I have found helpful in dealing with trouble in such a way that the Law of Challenge and Response becomes operative and the power of the Plus Factor comes through. Here are those five suggestions:

One: Face up to the problem.

There's always the temptation to shy away from it, to play ostrich, to bury your head in the sand, and hope the problem will go away. It probably won't. In fact, the longer you hide from it, the more menacing it becomes.

So stand up straight. Look the problem in the eye. Take its measure. Analyze it. Dissect it. Perhaps it isn't as formidable as it looks. Even if it is, say to yourself, 'All right. The challenge is here. I am going to respond to it. With God's help, and with the hidden Plus Factor within me, I can handle it.'

Two: Having taken a good hard look at the problem, take a good hard look at yourself.

Very often people find themselves in trouble because the trouble is really in them. People have come to me plagued by business or financial woes, only to find on closer discussion that they were carrying around such a load of guilt from moral transgressions that their thinking was impaired, their energy short-circuited, and their business judgment clouded. They were in trouble, all right, but before they could deal with it they had to recognize and deal with the trouble in themselves, the moral trouble that was preventing the Plus Factor from coming to their aid.

127

Three: Having faced up to the problem and examined yourself, take some kind of action.

Have you ever noticed how many of the majestic healing utterances of Jesus begin with a verb of action? 'Go and wash. . . .' 'Stretch forth thy hand. . . .' 'Take up thy bed. . . .' This surely is no accident. Action is a restorer and builder of confidence. Inaction is not only the result but the cause of fear. Perhaps the action you take will be successful; perhaps different action or adjustments will have to follow. But any action is better than no action at all. So don't wait for trouble to intimidate or paralyze you. Make a move. The Prodigal Son didn't make his way home by lying in the gutter. He moved!

Four: Don't be unwilling to ask for help.

Some people act as if trouble were a disgrace, something to be concealed at all costs. Others say grimly, 'It's my problem. I'll work it out by myself.' Such attitudes are a mistake. No one is completely self-sufficient; we all need help from time to time. In just about every area of trouble there are experts who are trained to help you: your doctor, your lawyer, your minister. Is your problem a fairly common one? Then in all likelihood there are organized groups of people who have been through the same mill and are willing to help you. People who have been alcoholics. Or compulsive gamblers. People who have retarded children. People who have lost their sight or their hearing. These are people who have faced trouble, who have survived it, and who stand ready to help others face it.

Even a sympathetic friend can help just by listening or offering a word of encouragement. Sharing trouble eases the strain and often helps perspective. I once knew an artist who ran into various difficulties. More than a little sorry for himself, he told a friend that he would never paint again, adding, 'Don't give me any platitudes or advice. It won't do any good. I'm through as a painter. I have too many troubles. I just can't see around them.' 'Well,' said the friend, 'I won't give you any advice, but I'll give you a definition of poetry that I once read. *Poetry is what Milton saw when he became blind.*' That was all the friend said, but the artist went back to his easel. He's a well-known watercolorist today.

Five: Don't fall in love with your trouble.

This last bit of advice seems to startle some people, but they are usually the ones who need it most. Painful though it is, trouble sometimes gives a kind of melancholy importance that can be very soothing to a shaky ego. It can also become a very convenient alibi for all sorts of failure and procrastination. Have you ever noticed how many people 'enjoy' poor health, talk about it, dwell upon it, make it the unhealthy center around which their lives revolve? Have you ever known people who, once they've made a mistake, refuse to move on, refuse to forget it?

This is no way to be. Troubles come. They also go. But you have to let them go! William James, the great psychologist, once said that the essence of genius lies in knowing what to overlook. Why not apply that to your troubles? Overlook the small ones, and when the big ones are ready to move on, open wide the door and let them go.

I believe what the Plus Factor is trying to teach us is this: Trouble can be unpleasant and painful and damaging, but it can also be the flint that strikes sparks out of the steel in your soul. The famous actor Walter

Hampden once was asked which sentence in the English language he considered the most memorable. He thought for a moment. Then he replied that in his opinion the greatest sentence was in an old Negro spiritual: 'Nobody knows the trouble I've seen; glory, hallelujah!'

Hampden was right: There is splendor in those words and wisdom too. They recognize that human life is full of pain and sorrow and suffering, but they don't stop with that mere recognition. They go on to express exultation. Those last two words ring with the magnificent conviction that there is something hidden in the spirit of man which, if called forth, can enable him to surmount trouble and suffering. Something that will turn defeat into victory.

That something is one of God's great gifts to mankind. It's the Plus Factor.

13

The Plus Factor and the Power of Prayer

What is the greatest power in the universe? Is it the enormous force of the hurricane or the tornado, or the tidal wave or the earthquake, or the exploding volcano? These are tremendous manifestations of nature's strength, but they are not the greatest power.

Is it man's discovery of the immense force that lies at the heart of the atom? This is a great wonder, but when you consider that this planet is just a speck of dust in the vast reaches of space, man's achievements with atomic energy are nothing but a little puff of smoke in the vastness of the cosmos.

What, then, is the greatest power in the universe? I believe that it is the mechanism by which man on earth establishes a connection that provides the flow of power between the mighty Creator and himself, between the great God who scattered the stars in the infinite night sky and the creature made in His own image: man. The flow of power between the Creator and man is the world's greatest power. It lies at the heart of the Plus Factor in human beings. And it is released and transmitted by means of a mechanism known as prayer.

Now when I say this, immediately you may feel let down because to you prayer may be nothing but pious words. It may be just a paragraph of sonorous language written in a book, or a string of hollow-sounding phrases uttered by a preacher, or some frantic last-minute plea for help in a crisis. These are superficial forms of this communication. But when this communication truly activates and liberates the Plus Factor in people, it has the power to change them.

In the Gospel of Saint Matthew we read, 'All things, whatsoever ye shall ask in prayer, believing, ye shall receive (Matthew 21:22). The key word, the word involving battle and struggle, is that word *believing*. Belief is hard doubt is easy. Anyone can doubt. It doesn't take brains or skill to doubt. But to cast your doubts aside and believe—ah, this requires stamina and resolution. And when you do believe, *really* believe, then impossibilities are overcome.

The reason I believe in the power of prayer is that over and over again I have seen what it can do for people. I know what it has done for me. To change a human being is the greatest feat imaginable, because the most complicated entity in the world is man himself. Man is riddled with contradictions, he is shackled with habit patterns, he has prejudices, he has resistances, he has complexities. He is the sum total of countless influences playing upon him since infancy. So when you talk about changing him, you know it will require some force of enormous power to do so.

But prayer has this power. For example, I was speaking one night in a big public hall in the Southwest. I arrived just in time for the meeting and went around to the stage entrance and onto a vast stage. There were some stagehands there, an electrician, and several other people. I noticed one man in particular. He immediately drew my attention because he was a picture of gloom and discouragement and despondency. He attracted my natural sympathy, so I went over and spoke to him.

He said, 'Doctor Peale, I came here tonight because I've read some of your books. I desperately need help. I'm so mixed up and conflicted and confused that I don't know what to do with myself or my problems. May I please talk with you right now?'

'Well,' I said, 'my friend, I'm going on stage here in about two minutes. But if you'll wait until I finish speaking, I promise you that I'll find time to talk with you about these things.'

I went on stage; I started speaking; I could see the man off in the wings. Then I got into my speech and forgot myself and everything else except the people out front.

When the speech was over, I remembered my man backstage. I went back, but he wasn't there. I said to the electrician, 'Where did that man go?' He said, 'He told me that he had to go home to relieve a baby-sitter.' 'Well, who is he?' I asked. 'I neglected to get his name.' The electrician knew his name. He added, 'He's quite a prominent lawyer in this city.'

I went back to my hotel. The man's number was in the book, so I called him on the telephone. 'Oh,' he said, 'thank you for calling.' I said, 'It's late, I know, but can't we talk over the phone?' He poured out such an accumulation of frustration and defeat and conflict in the next fifteen or twenty minutes that it would have touched a heart of stone. I could tell that he was an intelligent and well-educated man because of the way he spoke and the orderliness of his mind. Finally he said, 'The trouble is, I'm ashamed to admit it, but I can't handle all this trouble. And what is even worse,' he added, 'I can't handle myself. I'm at the end of my rope. I just don't know what to do.'

'Well,' I said to him, 'do you pray about this?'

'Oh,' he said, 'yes, I pray all the time. I'm always asking God to help me. I implore Him!' And the very way he said it revealed to me that he was full of fear and tension, he was full of frantic petition, he was hysterically demanding something of God.

I said, 'Well, if you don't mind my saying so, I think your prayers are wrong. When you get that panicky in your prayers you're closing off the interrelation between God and yourself. You're praying in such a tense manner that you're not letting go of the problem. The thing that God wants is a humble and a contrite spirit. So,' I said, 'let's pray right now. You tell the Lord you can't handle these problems so you're going to turn them over to Him.'

'Oh,' he said, 'I hate to be so spineless.'

I said, 'Be humble. Just tell the Lord you can't handle them. And tell the Lord you can't handle yourself. So, therefore, you surrender the problems and you surrender yourself into His hands.' And he said, 'Lord, I can't handle these problems. I give them to You. I cannot handle myself. I give myself to You. Thank You very much. Amen.'

I never saw the man from that day till this. But I hear from him occasionally. In that moment he found release, he found peace—not a complete answer for every problem, but in the days that followed, his fragmented personality flowed together again. He

134

became master of himself and, therefore, master of his problems. The Plus Factor began once more to work in him. Today he holds a position of trust as one of the honorable judges of his community, and he told me that whenever anybody comes before him who he feels needs this same treatment, he offers it to them. 'I give to them,' he says, 'the greatest secret in the world—that there truly is a power that can heal them and bring them together: 'All things, whatsoever ye shall ask in prayer, believing, ye shall receive' (Matthew 21:22).'

Now what does a person have to do to be on the receiving end of this power? The first step is to humble yourself and let go of the problem, leaving it in the hands of God. This kind of prayer is sometimes called the Prayer of Self-Effacement, and it unblocks the channels through which God's power can reach the person praying. Until you humble yourself and give yourself and your problem to God, you'll never get the answer you are seeking. But when you do, you will.

The second important step is to realize that prayer isn't just some neat exercise in words. It has to be deeper than that. Most people do not pray in depth; therefore, nothing happens.

I remember once being on a train with Roland Hayes, the black singer, one of the finest Christian gentlemen I have ever met. He told me that he'd built his whole life and his whole career on prayer. He was led into this way of life by his grandfather, who wasn't as well-educated as Mr. Hayes, but who had tremendous faith. The old man told Roland that the reason some prayers didn't seem to get anywhere was because 'they ain't got no suction.' That was the phrase his grandfather used, and that's quite a word: *suction*. He meant that some prayers don't go down to the level where they start pulling on the prayer, drawing him closer to God.

In my mind there's no doubt about it: the deeper the prayer, the more remarkable the results. A friend told me once of a young American wife who was all alone with her baby in a small manufacturing town in France. She had just gone over to join her husband who was representing an American company there. She did not speak the language, and she knew absolutely no one.

Just after she arrived, her husband was recalled to the States for an important conference that required an absence of several days. Soon after he left, the baby became ill with an acute respiratory infection. The child's fever mounted very rapidly. As night came on his breathing became more and more labored. None of the remedies the mother tried had any effect. She grew more and more terrified. The house was quite isolated. She did not know how to use the telephone. Even if she had known the name of a doctor, she would not have been able to make herself understood.

As the hours went by she paced the floor, holding the baby in her arms, tears of inner agony streaming down her face. Near midnight the child's fever rose so high that he went into a convulsion, a terrifying manifestation, as anyone who has seen one knows. His breath rattled feebly in his throat. The mother, convinced that her child was dying, fell on her knees by the bed and closed her eyes and cried, 'Oh, God, my baby is dying. Please, please hear me. I need Your help. I need it now. Save my baby, Lord; I know You can do it. I believe You can do it. I beg You to do it. Right now. This minute. This second. Please, dear Lord, in Jesus' name. Right now, Lord. Right now!'

She felt as if the prayer had been wrenched from the deepest part of her soul. The room seemed full of a ringing silence. And in the silence she heard a soft, sighing sound. It was her baby, breathing normally. She opened her eyes and looked at the baby's face. The flush of fever was gone. Only a light perspiration remained. The baby was sleeping as peacefully as if nothing had happened. But something *had* happened. The intensity of the mother's prayer had swept aside all barriers and touched the great compassionate heart of the Infinite. It had opened a channel to unlimited power, and as the power coursed through that channel it overwhelmed the disease that had the baby in its grip.

'I believe You can do it,' the mother said. *Believe.* That was the crucial element, the operative word that made the whole extraordinary happening possible. A mother fighting for her child's life, praying for him, desperately reaching out for the greatest Plus Factor of all—what greater 'suction' can there be?

Well, you may say, others have had serious illness, and others have prayed with deep sincerity and urgency, and yet no such instantaneous cure has been their reward. How do you account for that?

I don't account for it. I am just saying that some prayers seem to be more effective than others, and intensity—or depth—often seems to be present when these miraculous happenings take place.

I recall once discussing the miracles that are said to happen at the shrine at Lourdes in southern France with my old friend and colleague Dr. Smiley Blanton, a psychiatrist. He was also the possessor of one of the clearest and most practical minds that I have ever had the good fortune to encounter. He was a religious man himself; he had been brought up by strong-faithed people in his native Tennessee. So he was always interested in the spiritual aspects of life. He had heard about the miracles of healing reported at the little town of Lourdes, and he decided to make a personal visit there to see for himself. He wanted to observe the whole process from a strictly scientific, objective, medical point of view, and he did. He spent several weeks there, talking to local doctors, to people who had come seeking a cure, to some who were healed and some who were not.

He found, to begin with, that authentic cases of healing—cases accepted by the medical profession and the Catholic Church—were very rare. But he also found that they did occur. Evidence based on diagnoses and X rays before and after the patient's visit to Lourdes showed that in some cases—in cases of advanced tuberculosis and other organic illnesses—instantaneous cures did take place. Sometimes at the moment when the patient drank Lourdes water or was immersed in it, sometimes when no such tangible agent was involved but when prayers were being offered either by the patient or by others.

I remember Dr. Blanton saying that it was as if the time factor in the healing process was enormously accelerated, so that medical progress that might normally be expected to occur over a period of months or even years was somehow condensed into a second or a millisecond of time—a tremendous intensification of the Plus Factor deep inside the sick or dying person.

What Dr. Blanton was seeking, really, was a common denominator that might link these miraculous healings together. What, if anything, did each of these people have in common? That was the question he kept asking himself.

'And did you find an answer?' I remember asking him.

He thought for a moment, then he said, 'Well, if there was a common denominator, it was this: All those people were terminal in the sense that mentally and emotionally they had reached the end of the line. They had tried every human remedy, and every medical solution, and none had worked. They were at the point where they said to themselves, 'I give up. I quit. I can't fight anymore. I can't try anymore.' It was this moment of complete and absolute relinquishment that seemed to set the stage for the cure that followed. It was almost as if the struggles and strivings of the patient somehow impeded or blocked the flow of curative power.'

I'm convinced that this willingness to let go should be added to the conditions that favor the emergence of the Plus Factor. Maybe we shouldn't wait to be dying or half-dead before we say, humbly and reverently, 'I can't carry all the burdens of life by myself. I'm helpless without You, dear Lord. Please take my helplessness and in return give me Your strength.' Maybe we shouldn't even wait until things are going badly and problems begin to seem insurmountable. Maybe even on the brightest days, at the brightest times, when the Plus Factor seems strong and success is riding triumphantly on our shoulders, we should still pray that prayer of humility and relinquishment, saying, 'I am full of gratitude for all the favors. You have granted, all the good things You have given me, but still I know that without You I am ineffective.'

The greatest men this nation has ever known have always been quick to acknowledge their dependence on a Power greater than themselves, and quick to seek aid from that Power. Take Abraham Lincoln, for example, in my opinion the greatest of them all, the one through whose life the Plus Factor shone with an unsurpassed radiance.

Where did this homely, gangling, backwoods lawyer get the moral greatness and the unbelievable stamina that enabled him to prevent his nation from being torn asunder and gave him as well the strength to bring freedom to a great race of people? A friend of mine, Congressman Pettingill of Indiana, went down into Lincoln country one time and made an estimate of the height of the primeval trees among which Lincoln wandered as a boy, huge trees, with tops seeming to scrape the sky and, all around, the deep forest silences. Pettingill said that Lincoln went to school to this great environment amidst these silences, and that in them he found God and learned to pray. His were deep, soul-searching prayers with enormous suction in them.

During the height of the Civil War a well-known actor named Murdoch was an overnight guest at the White House. In the dead of night he was awakened by the sound of a voice, a voice in great distress and emotional agony. He crept out into the hall. He followed the sound of the voice and he looked through a door that was ajar. He said that he saw the tall, lanky form of Abraham Lincoln face down on the floor, his fingers digging into the carpet as he poured out his sense of in-sufficiency and inadequacy, asking Almighty God to help him save the Republic. And Murdoch said that at that moment all his doubts about the outcome of the war and about the future of the nation left him.

Belief is hard, doubt is easy.... It doesn't take brains to doubt.
But to cast your doubts aside and believe requires stamina and resolution.
And when you do believe, really believe, then impossibilities are overcome.

I believe that when prayer reaches such intensity, even the physical forces of nature may respond, just as Christ stilled the raging waters of the Sea of Galilee in a storm that threatened to sink the boat carrying Him and His disciples. I remember very well a story told a few years ago by Don Bell, a cowboy who lives in Wyoming. He had been brought up by his Aunt Mae, a widow who lived on a homestead in eastern Colorado. Aunt Mae had to fight dust storms and tornadoes and sometimes she and her four children were close to starvation. Grasshoppers came and devoured her small crops. She decided to get some turkeys to eat the grasshoppers, and they did; so she put all her small resources into raising turkeys. She had about two thousand turkeys, and she had to guard them day and night to make sure the coyotes didn't get them. She would take her Bible with her when she went into the fields to watch over the birds.

One day a sudden storm came up, black clouds, a vicious wind, and a hard hail thundering across the plains. Aunt Mae saw it coming. There was no time to drive the turkeys to shelter. She knew that the hail would wipe out the whole flock in a matter of minutes. Her young nephew, Don, was with her, and he wanted to run, but Aunt Mae said, 'We're not going anywhere, Don. We're staying with the birds.'

Here's how Don described what happened next: 'Aunt Mae just stood there with her Bible held to her chest and she watched that storm come on. I kept my eyes on her, watching for a sign that we should run, leave the birds, even if they were our last hope.

'But Aunt Mae would give no such sign, even though the wind threw tumbleweeds and stinging dirt at us. She opened her Bible and started shouting Scripture at the storm, 'Then they cry unto the Lord in their trouble,' she shouted out, 'and he bringeth them out of their distresses. He maketh the storm a calm, so that the waves thereof are still. Then are they glad because they be quiet so he bringeth them unto their desired haven.' The wind was whipping at her now and the pages of her Bible fluttered. But she went on: 'He blesseth them also, so that they are multiplied greatly; and suffereth not their cattle to decrease.' Aunt Mae was undaunted, defying the storm around her with holy words: 'Whoso is wise, and will observe these things, even they shall understand the loving-kindness of the Lord' (Psalms 107:28-30, 38, 43).

'The sign to run never came. Aunt Mae stood her ground, and in the end the storm passed safely to the north, to an unpopulated area. Only then did Aunt Mae take her eyes off that horizon. She bent her head and prayed. Only then did my fear leave me.'

What a magnificent scene, that weather-beaten pioneer woman standing tall in the path of the onrushing storm, clutching her Bible and *praying* that hail away from her precious turkeys!

But the Plus Factor that is released by prayer isn't limited to major crises. It can work in smaller ones no less dramatically. I have a friend, the head of a well-known boys' prep school. He told me that as a boy he worked in a foundry because he had decided to drop out of school. He changed his mind eventually, but by that time he was older than the other boys in his class. He had to struggle to make up the time lost. He said he did it 'by study and prayer.'

His mother, who was very devout, had made him promise that he would never study on Sunday, and he kept that promise. But the time came when the entrance examination in Greek was scheduled for 11 A.M. on Monday morning 'and it was all Greek to me,' he said.

He arose at 3 A.M. Monday morning and opened his Greek textbook. He said, 'Lord, I have an examination today at eleven o'clock. If you want me to go to college, please help me with this examination. I have only a few hours; tell me what to study.'

He said that the number of a page came into his mind. He turned to that page and began to study it. He studied it until he had memorized it. And when the time came, he found that the examination was based almost entirely on the page he had committed to memory.

This struck him as so remarkable that he told his professor about it.

'That's a very curious coincidence,' the professor said. 'I didn't make out that examination until eight o'clock Monday morning. Apparently you saw the idea even before it was in my mind. Mental transference, no doubt.'

'Excuse me, sir,' said this boy who was to become a headmaster, 'I believe it was more than that. God wanted to use me. He wanted me to continue my education. And so He put into my mind what He was going to put into yours.'

Can the Plus Factor do such things? I believe it can when it is focused and channeled and liberated by prayer.

The flow of power and the release of the Plus Factor that comes from prayer are available to all of us, but they can be blocked by a variety of things. Pride can be a block. Tension can be a block. Fear can be a block. Sin can be a block. Negative thinking can be a block.

Not long ago I gave a talk in a Texas city and afterward a man spoke to me. He said, 'Do you believe that prayer can work in practical business matters?'

I assured him that I did.

'Well,' he said, 'I moved here recently from another state. I own a house up there. I had to buy a house here in this city and I've been trying to sell my former home, but I haven't been able to move it. I've done everything I can think of, and I've asked God to help me, but the house isn't sold.'

I asked him what price he wanted for the house, and he told me. Then I asked him what a reasonable profit on the sale of the house would be. He told me, and the price he had placed on the house was a lot higher than that.

I said to him, 'I think the problem with selling this house may be that you are concerned only with yourself. How big is this house?'

'It's quite large,' he said. 'Large enough for a family with children.'

'Well,' I said, 'here's what I suggest that you do. Say to the Lord that He must have a family somewhere who needs this house, and ask Him to bring that family and your house together. You're going to think about that family enjoying that house of yours and you're going to stop thinking about yourself.'

He stared at me, and I could tell that he was quite astonished.

I said, 'Pray that they will find the house, and when they do, you'll explore their financial situation and work things out so that they can buy the house. When you approach it in this way, you'll eliminate the selfishness that may be blocking your prayers and I think God's will may be done.'

The man just nodded his head and went away. About two weeks later I had a letter from him. It said, 'Believe it or not, I did exactly as you suggested. The nicest young family you ever saw with three small children loved my house. They said they had been praying and describing the house they needed to the Lord, and suddenly they were led to this house and when they saw it they knew it was exactly what they wanted because it was exactly as they had pictured it in their prayers.

His letter went on: 'They didn't have much money, but they did have enough for a down payment. I checked their credit, and it looked good. Anyway, they're happy, and I'm happy, and maybe I didn't make a lot of profit but I discovered something much more important. I discovered that prayer works when you align yourself with the power of God, and that's what I intend to do from now on. Thank you!'

The key to successful living, to happiness, to everything is to saturate your mind and your plans and your hopes and your dreams with prayer. That is what we do at the Foundation for Christian Living in Pawling, New York, which had its start years ago when my wife, Ruth, began mailing out copies of my sermons to a few interested people. Now it reaches nearly one million people all over the world, mailing thirty million pieces of literature annually. *Guideposts* magazine, which we started forty years ago on a wing and a prayer, you might say, is a publishing phenomenon with over four million subscribers and read by nearly sixteen million persons monthly.

Sometimes prayer liberates the Plus Factor in delightful and unexpected ways. I remember once meeting a woman in Pittsburgh who had an interesting story to tell. She said, 'I'm thirty-four years of age. My husband died about a year ago from cancer. Not long ago one of my children was badly burned by grease from the stove. I have taken him to doctors, of course, but my money is running out.' She went on to say that she had worked for a store, but it had gone out of business. And the insurance company had never paid on her husband's death because in the last days of his illness he had neglected to pay a premium and the policy had lapsed. 'Now,' she said to me, 'you always talk about positive thinking. What would you say in my case?'

I said, 'The first thing I suggest is that you take all these problems and put them in the Lord's hands and ask Him for guidance, He will clear your thinking and give you creative ideas, restore hope, energy and confidence in you.' And I added, 'We might as well start right now. Let's pray together about this problem.'

She was a good woman. I still remember how earnestly she recommitted her life to Christ. Finally she said, 'You know, it's a strange thing, but as we were praying I got the idea that I should go to see the manager of my husband's insurance company.

She tried and tried to see this manager, but the receptionist, who was familiar with the case and who had decided that the manager would do nothing about it, refused to let her in. But she kept trying, and one day when the receptionist was away from her desk, she walked into the manager's office. She sat down and apologized to him for 'barging in like this.' 'But,' she said, 'I have prayed most earnestly about this matter, and the Lord told me to come and see you.' And she proceeded to outline the case.

The manager got out the file. He said, 'I'll study this. Come back tomorrow.' When she returned the next day, he said, 'There's no legal obligation to pay in this matter. But your husband paid his premiums faithfully for many years, and I think there may be a moral obligation. So I am going to recommend that this policy be paid.' Then he said, 'And what else can I do?'

She told him about her son, and he went to work on proper hospitalization and care for the boy. And that was taken care of. Then he said, 'And what else can I do?' She told him about her unemployment and he helped her get another job. All this took several months. Then again he said, 'And what else can I do for you?' 'Why, nothing,' she said. 'You've been very helpful and kind. I do appreciate it.'

'Well,' he said, 'there's something you can do for me. You're a widow and I'm a widower. I would like very much to marry you. Will you marry me?'

And so they were married, and are living happily together to this day—certainly one of the most astonishing results I ever had from praying with anybody!

Do you want this kind of Plus Factor to manifest in your life? Then learn to pray in depth, with 'suction,' with all the power of belief. And then prepare yourself for great things. Because miracles can happen.

14

Putting Enthusiasm to Work

*E*nthusiasm is a superimportant, basic element in successful living. The 'alive' type of personality always goes places when that aliveness is accompanied by positive thinking and solid faith.

Take, for example, the following letter from a distinguished professor in a leading university:

Dear Dr. Peale:

Through your work you have touched my life. Allow me to expand on this.

Born of European immigrant parents, I grew up in Paraguay, South America. While my schoolmates wore shoes and socks, I wore sandals. But poverty was felt only in material possessions— my parents placed great emphasis on teaching lasting values. During my teenage years my father introduced me to your book *The Power of Positive Thinking*, whose teachings he applied by encouraging me to think big. He scraped up enough money to get me a (one-way) ticket to

149

study in the United States. I would not return home again for another six years.

During the first semester in college I kept in a drawer my entire monetary assets: 5 cents! So, while at the age of 19 I learned English, my third language, I took course work and also worked as a janitor and waiter. But I had a goal, and your work is helping me achieve it.

Today I am married to a wonderful wife, and have three beautiful children. I am professor at a major midwestern university with a Ph.D. in chemistry. The student body of 23,000 has voted me 'Top Educator,' and I am recipient of the Indiana University state-wide Lieber Award for Distinguished Teaching. I have traveled all over the world serving as consultant to the Ford Foundation and the Asian Development Bank. I operate a publishing firm and own a considerable amount of real estate. I have served my church by leading our congregation through a million dollar building project.

I am writing these things not to boast, but to acknowledge the tremendous power locked within human beings, which, when properly catalyzed, will flourish beyond belief. You and your work have served as beautiful catalysts. Thank you!

Cordially yours,
Erwin Boschmann, Ph.D.

Let's look at the factors that worked in this man's personality that contributed to his success. He did not grow bitter in poverty. He was not a griper. Lasting values were taught to him and he responded to those values.

He learned to think big and he had a goal which he set out to achieve against great odds: no money and the necessity of mastering a new language.

He possessed boundless enthusiasm and was a committed Christian with the power of faith working in him. Added to all this was positive thinking, and the net result is a great and successful life. Obviously he has the Plus Factor in full measure.

I want to point out that enthusiasm releases and feeds the Plus Factor that is inherent within you. That factor may not be very strong or effective at the moment. But it can become so and one way to activate it into a powerful force is to have enthusiasm going for you, real, contagious enthusiasm.

'But' you may say, 'what if you don't have enthusiasm? You can't be enthusiastic if you are lacking enthusiasm. And you cannot buy it in a drugstore in the form of a pill or a liquid, So you are out of luck, for if you just do not have enthusiasm you cannot be an enthusiastic person.'

The answer to that doleful complaint and excuse is, 'Oh, yes, you can!' All you have to do is practice the 'as if' principle. This is one of the most powerful methodologies that can be employed by the person who really wants to do something with himself or herself.

And just what is the 'as if' principle? I think it was first stated by Professor William James, sometimes called the father of American psychological science. If you want to cultivate a desired attitude, you may do so by acting as if you had it. If, for example, you are a person of fear and you want instead to be a person of courage, you proceed to act courageously. In due course if you persist in acting as if you had courage, you will ultimately become a courageous person. Now please do not reject this truth and say it isn't so. Remember it was put forth by one of the foremost scholars in American history. And it has been proved to be effective by many people. One of them is the author of this book. I, personally, believe in the 'as if' principle because I have used it and found that it works.

In my younger years I was the victim of an enormous inferiority complex. And as is common among people so afflicted, I practiced the 'as if' principle, but in reverse; for I acted as if I were a nobody with no ability. And so naturally I developed into a sadly defeated person. I became exactly as I acted. Then through various felicitous circumstances I took on the characteristics of a positive thinker and began to practice the 'as if' principle.

When a person develops enthusiasm, exciting things begin happening. From then on that individual is very likely to become different, perhaps markedly so. If previously he or she was lethargic, lacking in drive and forcefulness, the metamorphosis of enthusiasm can be dramatic indeed. A hitherto unimaginative, sleepy man or woman suddenly comes alive, is revitalized, and moves up and on to a success previously undreamed of by anyone, including himself.

Actually, enthusiasm is one of the most effective activation agents. It gets people and results going— really going—and in ways that are often spectacular. As in the case of a young Toronto taxi driver.

I had a friend some years ago in Toronto. He was a chemist by profession, though on Sundays he was the teacher of the largest Bible class in Canada. Dr. Albert E. Cliffe was a highly motivated man and crowds flocked to hear him talk, for he was an outstanding conveyor of enthusiasm for what people could be.

One March morning, when a stormy gale was sweeping the city, Al Cliffe hailed a taxi in Toronto. To the glum and somewhat surly young driver he said a cheery good morning. 'Wonderful day, isn't it?' And it was just that, for any day was wonderful to Al. 'You should have your head examined,' snarled the driver. 'What do you mean a wonderful day with this lousy weather!' Then he added, 'This country is on the way out. No opportunity here anymore; nothing any good.'

Cliffe let the young man empty himself of his gripes and complaints, then he asked kindly, 'What's the matter, son?'

This really set the young fellow off. It was soon after the war. The boy said, 'I'm a war veteran, gave three years to my country, but what's the country doing for me? I can't get a job in my line. I'm a graduate engineer. I walked the streets of my own city finally taking this job, a taxi driver. I'm disgusted, fed up, completely turned off.'

Cliffe said, 'My friend, do you want to know what will get you off this negative dead centre and start you going?'

'I'd sure like to know what,' the driver snorted. 'Now don't discount what I'm going to say. It's enthusiasm that will turn things around for you—real enthusiasm—the genuine article.'

At this the driver turned around suddenly to stare at his passenger, nearly running up on the curb. 'Enthusiasm,' he expostulated. 'Aw, come off it, mister. What is there to be enthusiastic about anyway?'

'Life,' answered Cliffe. 'It's wonderful to be alive and young as you are. Add up your assets. Your future is out there ahead of you, and don't write Canada off either. It's a great land and you and I live in one of the finest cities in the world.'

The young driver listened. 'Where did you get all this enthusiasm, sir?'

Cliffe's reply was brief, in only two words: 'Jesus Christ.'

'I was a believer once, too,' the driver said. 'Become one again, son, Think enthusiasm, act out enthusiasm, talk enthusiasm, and you will become enthusiastic. Then you will go places and life will become exciting.'

About two years later this young taxi driver went to see Dr. Cliffe. 'You really got to me that morning,' he said. 'It wasn't altogether what you said, although that made sense. It was also what you are. And that struck me. Well,' he continued, 'I gave it a lot of thought and I did as you said. I deliberately tried to make myself enthusiastic. As I did that, I realized I was getting more fun out of driving a taxi.'

Then he went on, 'One day I picked up a fare at the Royal York Hotel. This man wanted to go to the airport. Believe it or not, it was another rainy day, but I told this man that every day is a good day and spoke with enthusiasm about the country and engineering, in which I was trained, and to which I was going to return one day.

'And do you know what this man said? It went something like this: "With the cheerful outlook you have and your outgoing personality, you shouldn't be driving a taxi. You say you are trained in engineering? Where did you go to school?" So I told him and he

154

invited me to come to see him at his office to talk about a possible job in his organization. "I like enthusiastic people working for me," he said, "when they are organized and have enough know-how. So come along and we'll check out your education and if all is okay, we will get you started."

'Well,' concluded the former taxi driver, 'I guess I'm doing okay. I've had two promotions. And I love it.'

When he told me this story, Al Cliffe, who as stated earlier was himself a scientist, commented, 'There's a lot more in most people than shows. Sometimes enthusiasm will bring it out, as in this case.'

To the important Plus Factor add enthusiasm, intellectual competency, as well as sound spiritual thinking, and you've got an unbeatable combination. You have the makings of somebody special.

America was made by the greatest assembly of enthusiasts the world has ever seen. All of those thousands who trekked west to settle new lands beyond the horizon were enthusiastic or they wouldn't have had the motivation to subject themselves to hardship and danger to make their dreams come true.

The United States despite its problems offers more opportunity for a person who wants to go places and do things than any other country on the globe. This is not an unsupported claim, for I have been on speaking trips from South America to Australia, from Singapore to Tokyo and, believe me, ours is still the land of opportunity.

I personally grew up among motivated, inspired, and enthusiastic people. And we had not yet become cynical. No one had taught us to regard enthusiasm as corny. I believe this cynical attitude came to be called sophistication, which seems an improper use of the word, for *sophistication* according to the dictionary means 'to know your way around the world.' And it is certainly not worldly wise to play yourself and opportunity down to the extent that it bypasses you. Even today the real achievers are excited, enthusiastic participants and leaders in creativity. In fact, to be with it in America today, increasingly one has to be an enthusiastic believer in incredible possibilities.

I really think the forefathers would be proud of us. They would see the old spirit of opportunity still at work in the nation they founded. As long as young men and women still are motivated, still follow their dreams, continue to believe in the future, the country is all right, very much all right. I've seen them in a hundred cities at huge motivational meetings— dreamers, thinkers, achievers—all wanting to go places and do things just as their forefathers did before them. And they have the same faith in God, the same faith in their country and in themselves. For them enthusiasm makes the difference, a great big difference in their happiness and achievement.

They would appreciate the story I'm about to relate. Though it happened fifty or more years ago, it is still pertinent, for the process is continuously modern.

Harry Moore lived with his widowed mother in Jersey City in three rooms in a run-down neighbourhood. They were very poor people but clean, decent, and church going. One day after school Harry came disconsolately into the kitchen, which doubled as a living room, sailed his cap onto a hat rack in the corner (all boys wore caps those days), and sprawled into a chair. His mother was stirring something that was cooking on the stove.

'Mama,' he said, 'I sometimes have strange feelings. They're funny. I get 'em every once in a while.'

'What kind of feelings, son?'

'Oh, I dunno, but it's like something inside of me keeps saying I'm somebody or can be something. I just don't know what it all means.'

'I do, Harry. I know exactly what it means. God is preparing you to be a great man sometime.' This simple woman had never heard of the Plus Factor in people, but she had enough sensitivity to know when it was stirring in a boy's mind.

'But, Mama, I can never amount to anything. We are poor and we have no pull or anything. Only the rich and famous can get to the top.'

Mama stopped stirring and pointed the dripping ladle at him, drops falling unheeded to the floor. 'Listen to me, son. Don't ever let me hear you talk like that again. All you need is just two things—God and gumption.'

Gumption is an old-fashioned word meaning common sense and the guts to go out and do something with yourself with enthusiasm and character. Gumption was the stuff of which sturdy, persistent, enthusiastic people were made. It's still a mighty good expression.

Years later when Harry was serving one of his three terms as governor, he was making a speech about America and its opportunity. He was a terrific speaker, with know-how and enthusiasm. Afterward a young fellow came up and said, 'Guy, I don't buy that stuff you were handing out. You know as well as I do that unless you've got money and pull and connections you can't get anywhere in this capitalist society.

That's why I've about decided to join the communists. They've got a program for us poor people.'

'Guess you don't know who you're talking to,' answered the governor. 'I talked just that way to my mother when I was a kid, all except that communist bit. I never was that dumb, poor as we were.' He told about the God and gumption advice. 'Okay, son, what is your goal?'

The boy had one. 'I want to be the best surgeon in this state.'

'Great,' said Governor Moore. 'What you can conceive you can achieve. Go with God and gumption.'

A few years later Governor A. Harry Moore gave the commencement talk at a large university on his usual theme, 'You Can Be What You Want to Be.' After the ceremony a graduate wearing the green hood of a new doctor of medicine came up and said, 'Hello, Guy. Remember me? Thanks to you I made it. That God and gumption bit did it.'

Telling me this story a long while after it happened, the governor commented, 'Get a person to have enthusiasm and all the other necessary qualities for success are activated—things like a goal, persistence, ability to work hard, determination to study.

'Then,' he said, 'you know something? God the Creator put an extra something into all of us. Some people let that something atrophy. But when enthusiasm gets to working, that extra quality develops and grows.' How right he was! He didn't name that extra quality to which he referred, but what he was talking about was clearly the Plus Factor as we term it.

The most unlikely person may have a huge Plus Factor inside of him. You don't know what a big Plus Factor may be right there within yourself. If you believe it is in you (and that is the first thing to do about it), you will then be ready for the second thing and that, of course, is to develop it and to grow it big— by being enthusiastic about your own potential.

I once knew a man who was considered the most knowledgeable man in the world about radio. And this same man had perhaps the most to do with creating the television industry. At about this time my home radio wasn't working well; so I called in a neighbourhood repairman who spent a long time tinkering with it and finally got it going. 'I suppose you know all about radio,' I said admiringly. 'Sure I do,' he cockily asserted. 'It's simple. Nothing to it.'

A short time later I was with the friend who was considered the greatest authority on radio. 'It's still a mystery to me,' he explained modestly, 'that we can actually transmit the human voice through what we call air waves. It's a miracle.' His face glowed with an expression of wonder. 'I've had enthusiasm since I was a small boy and that enthusiasm has grown to enormous proportion as I have worked with radio and television.'

The man to whom I'm referring is the late David Sarnoff, longtime head of the Radio Corporation of America and founder of the National Broadcasting Company. He had a built-in Plus Factor that was activated by enthusiasm, and it was a spectacular Plus Factor. You wouldn't think would you that a young Jewish boy born in Russia, son of poverty-stricken immigrants, growing up in the old Hell's Kitchen in New York City would actually have the Radio

Corporation of America and the National Broadcasting Company tucked away inside of him as a Plus Factor? But such is the romantic possibility of human beings. When I think of David Sarnoff, a statement of the German philosopher Nietzsche sometimes comes to mind: 'Nothing ever succeeds which exuberant spirits have not helped to produce.' David Sarnoff possessed enthusiasm in abundance, and exciting things happen when a person has a burning and unextinguishable enthusiasm.

The Plus Factor requires enthusiasm, for it is that which keeps the individual carrying on in pursuit of a goal. Enthusiasm is what insures the dogged, never-give-up, hang-in-there attitude. As long as enthusiasm is strongly sustained, the extra something within a person that we call the Plus Factor may be counted on to function, and if necessary over great odds. Harvey J. Berman in his magnificent description of the courageous swimming by Florence Chadwick of the English channel from England to France declares that it was the most remarkable attempt ever made on the difficult channel. She came close to death. Agonizing cramps gripped first her legs, then her stomach. She became lost as night descended over the sea. But nothing deterred her, she explained: 'There was nothing else to do but go on, so I did.'

Sixteen hours after she entered the channel on the English side she stumbled onto the beach in France to be labeled 'the greatest female swimming star of all time.' How did she accomplish this astounding feat? Her explanation, 'With God's patient help.' And she had a motto that also helped. 'Winners never quit; quitters never win.'

Beyond all these great assets Florence Chadwick had, within her a Plus Factor, which she developed into an extraordinary source of power. And a burning enthusiasm for swimming fired that Plus Factor, keeping the heat on at all times. So she was able to carry on, and to keep carrying on to the victorious end. And that, incidentally, is what each of us must do: Just keep it going, always going until we cross the goal line. And it is a fact that enthusiasm is the power that keeps us in the swim or race or struggle all the way to the end. If you keep your enthusiasm up, you will never even contemplate giving up.

After reading the foregoing human demonstrations of the power of the Plus Factor motivated by enthusiasm, you may very well raise the question, 'Just how may I increase my enthusiasm?' In anticipation of that question I made a list of a few ways that enthusiasm may be developed and increased.

Six Steps to Developing Enthusiasm

1. As stated earlier, employ the as-if principle; act as if you had enthusiasm and it will tend to develop in your mind. I repeat this for the simple reason that it is so effective.

2. Practice being enthusiastic about simple things. For example, 'Look at those fleecy clouds against a blue sky. Isn't that beautiful?' or 'Honey, I never tasted a more delicious dinner. You surely are a terrific cook!' You might also admire the nicely cut green lawn or the purring sound of your car motor as you pull out into the roadway. Enthusiasm for the simple things will add up to a general attitude of enthusiasm.

3. Tell yourself every morning as you go to work that you love your job. Think of it as interesting, even

fascinating. By so doing you will ultimately get enthusiastic about your work—and you will undoubtedly do a better job.

4. Daily, as you board a bus, train, or subway, tell yourself that you really like people. Do this even when they push and shove you. Look for the interesting and likeable qualities in people. Act toward them as if you were enthusiastic about them. In due course, they will become enthusiastic about you.

5. Every morning say aloud a Scripture verse such as: 'This is the day which the Lord hath made; we will rejoice and be glad in it'. Another good one is: 'Surely goodness and mercy shall follow me all the days of my life'. You'll get to loving God and when you love God, you love life—you become an enthusiast. That is the way it works.

6. See how many 'wonderful things' you can identify daily: a spectacular sunset; the face of an old man rugged as a granite cliff; a dogwood tree in full bloom; snow drifted high against an old stone wall. As you emphasize the wonder of life, you will develop that wonder of the attitude called enthusiasm. And you, too, will become more wonderful.

As you do these exercises, and other enthusiasm-developing acts that you yourself will think of, that extra special something in your nature that we call the Plus Factor will grow and you will grow along with it.

People today are health conscious. They want their bodies to be stronger, healthier. And so they diet, exercise, walk, jog, run—and this is all to the good. To perhaps a lesser degree, people work with their minds to make them stronger, more knowledgeable, more efficient. They read mind-developing material. Education embraces the old as well as the young and adult education flourishes.

But it is development in the area of the spirit where we are perhaps the weakest. If the spiritual nature is to grow and develop, spirit no less than body and mind needs exercise and thoughtful nurture. The quality of enthusiasm is basically of the spirit, although it is easier to be enthusiastic when the body is healthy and the mind is fine tuned. Thus it is that the holistic principle of body, mind, and spirit is today regarded as increasingly important. It greatly contributes to a general upgrading of one's life, giving to it deeper meaning, enjoyment, and excitement, and is a powerful releasing agent of the Plus Factor.

But there is a method for developing enthusiasm and thereby releasing your Plus Factor, a method superior in my judgment to any other that may be employed. This method is bypassed by some people for what is really an irrational reason. They are mentally and emotionally set against it, because some person they don't like used it; or they had an unhappy experience with someone who taught it; or they encountered unattractive forms of it; or they just don't understand it. What I'm referring to is what I call the Christian-experience method. This, in brief, is the establishment of a definite personal relationship with Jesus Christ as your Lord, your Savior, your friend. A relationship so close and real that He is with you every day helping you in everything.

It creates a new life-style—as if you had been born all over again, this time as a new person. People who have this tremendous experience are the outstanding enthusiasts of this world. For them everyday life is more and more wonderful. Things that once threw them, defeated them, and made them disgusted and surely can now be overcome. They rise above problems, or throw them out of the way, or know how to live with them successfully.

'But,' you may ask, 'just how do you find this wonderful new life?' There are many ways, but one I recommend is to read the four Gospels—Matthew, Mark, Luke, and John. Read them at one sitting if you can, or at least read large sections at a time. By so doing, you will encounter the most fascinating personality of all time, One who is alive and helping people today, not merely a figure of the dull past. You will find what His teachings really are and how they make much sense. You will become aware that He outlines a way of life that really works and that leads to joy and victory.

You may be quite astonished as you read, astonished that anyone could so succinctly and with such amazing clarity articulate the basic truth about life. Some may even exclaim, 'Is this Christianity? I thought it was theological arguments, conflicts between groups, each of which presumes they alone have the truth. I thought it was anything but this plain, aim pie though moving statement of the way life is at its best.'

As you get to know the center of it all, which is Jesus, a strange and marvelous transformation will come over you. He will remove your inner conflicts, heal your hurts, do away with your resentments, strengthen you against your weaknesses, and fill your mind with peace such as you have never known. A new and amazing sense of power will surge through you and you will find yourself able to do things as never before. As the

Plus Factor in you is released, an enthusiasm such as you have never experienced will signal the astounding change in you.

Just how can I know this can happen to you? Because it happened to me and I've seen it occur with amazing results in many persons across the years. Because I believe this tremendous experience should not be denied to others who are still stumbling along, being defeated at the same old roadblocks when they do not need to, I am writing this book called *Power of the Plus Factor*.

One night I was speaking at a motivational sales rally in a city in western Canada. Several thousand people were present, most of them in sales. I judged that the average age of the large audience was no more than thirty. All seemed imbued with the desire to get ahead in their respective businesses. That everyone present had a definite desire for self-improvement was indicated by their serious but enthusiastic attitude. I spoke on the subject of 'Enthusiasm Makes the Difference' and pointed out that an enthusiastic attitude is an important ingredient in success.

After the speech I returned to my hotel and walking to the elevator, I was accosted by a nice-looking young man who told me that he had followed me from the hall because he wanted to discuss something of a personal nature. His problem, he said, was desultoriness. He just couldn't care less about anything, including his work. He knew his attitude was very wrong and wouldn't lead to success, but he had not been able to do anything about it. As a matter of fact, he said he hadn't cared enough to make an effort to correct himself.

But he told me that my message that night on enthusiasm had really reached him and disturbed him. For the first time he realized that he had no future unless he changed from his desultory attitude and became an excited, enthusiastic person. This change would require a miracle he asserted, and he doubted very much that it would happen. 'But,' he concluded, 'for the first time in my life I want to change.'

I told him that the desire to change was the first step. 'Intensity of desire is the beginning of the process of becoming different,' I declared and offered the opinion that he was ready for something great to happen to him.

'I know I've got to become outgoing, enthusiastic, even excited if I am to go further toward real success, but how can this happen to an apathetic, uninterested guy like me? That's the sixty-four-dollar question,' he concluded dejectedly.

'What's your name, my friend?'

'Oh, just call me Freddie,' he replied.

This conversation lasted perhaps ten minutes, and during it we stood in a rather busy hotel lobby. 'Well, Freddie, I will level with you. It's not easy to effect change in a personality where disinterest has long been prevalent. Something dramatically acute is necessary to cause definite change. You may have to spend a long time unlearning defeatist mental habits. But,' I said, 'there is one way in which a healing therapy can take place almost instantly. It requires that intensity of desire I spoke of, plus an admission you can do nothing for yourself, and finally a complete commitment to Jesus Christ. If it is His will to release you immediately, He can do it. But He may instead put you through the long process of unlearning and relearning new mental habits. The only thing to do is just to ask Him, that's all.'

'I understand,' he said and he thanked me. We shook hands and said good night. I never saw this man thereafter but a year or so later at a convention a man said, 'I've a message for you. Freddie said to tell you it worked. And also to tell you he will always love you for pointing the way. I might add,' he concluded, 'that Freddie is one of our top producers. He is a ball of fire, with enthusiasm.'

Freddie's Plus Factor was released and enthusiasm became a renewing force in his life and business experience. And the same can happen to anyone who will employ the unfailing method which I gave that night to Freddie. He was smart enough to accept it and go with it.

15

Becoming an Achiever

*J*ust what is an achiever? What image comes to mind when the word *achiever* is mentioned?

Probably to most people the term means a person who accumulates big money, or rises to a high executive status in industry or to stardom in television or the movies or politics. Such a person is indeed an achiever. But like other words in the English language, the word *achiever* has been somewhat distorted from its original and basic meaning.

Here is its definition in my dictionary: to achieve is 'to accomplish something: attain an objective.' Achievement is defined as 'something accomplished, especially by valor, skill, or exertion; a feat; exploit; the act of achieving.'

By these definitions it would seem that simple, unheralded people who never have any publicity, the plain workers of the world who accomplish something worthwhile, are also achievers. In fact, taken together these achievers can well be acclaimed the builders and preservers of our country just as much as the celebrities whose names and pictures are constantly before the public.

The Plus Factor is just as available to these unsung achievers as it is to the more publicized ones. I doubt if my Uncle Will ever got his name in the paper, unless it was printed in the Lynchburg, Ohio, weekly paper as one of the graduates of Lynchburg High School. But he had the Plus Factor and the Plus Factor had him. You see, William Fulton Peale was a poor boy, and anything he attained he had to work for. He was a born salesman. He could sell anything to anyone. That was because he always sold good products, he was thoroughly honest and had an outgoing friendly way about him.

After high school he got a job selling house to house in the rural districts of Tennessee, and as he sold he left behind him a trail of friends. He worked his way through the University of Tennessee, graduating with honours. 'Pa never had to put down a cent to get me through college,' he used to say proudly.

Later he taught at a school in Tennessee and in this work he was equally successful. 'Teaching is selling,' he declared, 'getting young people to buy constructive knowledge to enable them to do great things with their lives.'

Young people loved him. 'He inspired and motivated me as no other teacher ever did,' a prominent businessman told me years later. 'Before I met him I had no belief in myself,' he added. 'He made me believe I had something extra inside of me.' Seems that Uncle Will was activating Plus Factors in his students. I know that this must have been true for he had the same effect upon me and I never sat in his classes.

He was always reaching out to do more with his own life. Talents were constantly spilling out of his personality. And he had the important ability to organize and constructively employ his talents. Thus it was that some people who had land in a growing area of Iowa heard of him. They approached him with the idea of selling this land to householders for home sites. Uncle Will would go into a community and announce a week of lot sales by auction. A plot would be laid out with graded streets and staked-off lots. Uncle Will always insisted that mature trees be saved to ensure a parklike neighbourhood.

He took me along during summer vacations to measure the lots, drive the stakes, and paint them. He gave prizes to attract buyers. He would always have a grand prize, a car, and he gave gold pieces as minor prizes (they were in common circulation then). And he passed out hundreds of one-pound boxes of candy. He drew enormous crowds. Prizes were by drawing and the fortunate person had to be present to receive his prize. Names went back into the box for the grand-prize drawing on the last day of the sale. The crowds stayed with him all through the heat of the Iowa summer.

I have heard some of the greatest orators of America from William Jennings Bryan to the present, but as a speaker I will put Uncle Will right up there with the best of them. I can see and hear him over the mist of years standing before those vast crowds telling those wonderful Iowa farmers what a home means. He drew a picture of the American homestead that brought tears to the eye. He pictured little children playing around the door and on the lawn, then in the golden years a man and wife walking hand in hand under the venerable trees. And he meant every word of it.

His great voice with no benefit of loudspeaker rang over the big crowd. They knew he was one of them, out of a common background of straitened circumstances, a motivated man who loved every one of his hearers and was persuading them to have a piece of America's soil in which to put down roots. And they bought those parcels by the hundreds. It has been sixty years since those exciting days, but whenever the word *achiever* is spoken I think of one of the greatest achievers I ever knew, my creative, innovative, indomitable, lovable Uncle Will.

What were the principles by which he became an achiever? Here they are:

On Becoming an Achiever

1. He believed that his country is the land of opportunity.
2. He wanted to make something of himself. He did not want to stay poor.
3. Money was never his god. He had no god but the Lord Almighty to whom he was ever faithful.
4. He knew one has to think to be an achiever and he did think. He also knew one has to work and he did work. He loved to work.
5. He liked people and they liked him.
6. He had boundless enthusiasm.
7. He had the ability to dream and turn many of his dreams into reality.
8. To him life was romantic and wonderful.
9. Above all, he never stopped trying. He never gave up.

Robert W. Service in 'The Quitter' sums up the spirit of persistence:

It's easy to cry that you're beaten and die;
It's easy to crawfish and crawl;
But to fight and to fight
When hope's out of sight
Why, that's the best game of all.
And though you come out of each grueling bout
All broken and beaten and scarred—
Just have one more try. It's dead easy to die;
It's the keeping on living that's hard.

I might add that to keep going as the poet so well describes is to have the Plus Factor aiding you in every trouble and every failure and disaster. If you do that, you will be able ultimately to turn every failure and indeed every disaster into an asset and achieve success.

An achiever is also a person who deals in quality. Actually he is himself of quality. He brings something good to other people. There is no phony element in the true and lasting achiever.

Whenever I think about the importance of quality in achievement, my old friend Joe Edison comes to mind. When I was young and single living in Syracuse, New York, where I was a pastor, one evening I found a little restaurant on a side street. It looked clean and attractive and since I was ready for dinner, I entered and climbed up on a stool at the counter. A man obviously of Middle Eastern extraction appeared out of the kitchen and when he saw me, a big smile came over his face. 'Welcome, Reverend Peale, welcome,' he said.

'You know me?' I asked in some surprise.

'Oh, yes,' he replied. 'I worship at your church. You see, I'm a Christian and go to church every Sunday.'

'What's your name?'

'Well, I'll give you my American name. My Lebanese name might be difficult for you. It's Joe Edison. Call me Joe for short. Now I'll fix you a beautiful steak.'

So saying he disappeared behind the swinging doors. Presently he emerged with the same big smile wreathing his face, and set a steak before me as though he was giving me a rare treasure. And it was a treasure indeed, the most delicious steak I had ever tasted. He stood watching me, fully expecting the admiration I was soon expressing. 'It's the best,' he said as one stating a fact, 'the best in central New York, maybe the best in the whole state. I buy only the best western beef. My motto is quality, only top quality, always the best.'

I got to know Joe very well as I dined at his restaurant at least twice a week. 'What is your goal, Joe?' I asked one night.

His eyes sparkled. 'It's to have the best quality restaurant anywhere. I love to cook. I don't want a chain, for I want to do the cooking myself.' Joe came out of poverty in Lebanon, arriving in this country with close to nothing. Now he was moving up on the leverage of quality.

Came the day when Joe moved to the West Coast, where in time he achieved his ideal restaurant. His dream came true. Often over the years when I found myself in his area, I would go to his place. No longer was it a counter with stools. It was not large, but it was a place of beauty. Joe would embrace me, 'My, but it's good to see you. Now you just sit here and

Joe will fix you a nice steak.' And it would be of the same delicious quality. It was cooking that never got better, for it was the best from the start. Joe would hover over me lovingly as I ate. He raised a fine family and became a substantially successful man, rising to the top of his profession on the wings of quality and loving-kindness. Joe was one of the achievers I've known in whose career the Plus Factor was uppermost. He is gone now, but there is still one grateful old customer who lovingly remembers him and salutes him as a top achiever, one who accomplished his goal.

On a recent trip to Europe *The International Herald Tribune* newspaper was delivered to my hotel room. A bold headline across three columns read, 'The Fading American Dream.' 'Never,' I said. 'Never is the American dream going to fade, not as long as we have men and women like those mentioned in this chapter and thousands more too numerous to mention here. These are achievers, the American way.

The Plus Factor, that extra power source built into each of us, is of superimportance, for achievers often have to pass through dark days and harsh experiences. What is necessary then is the courage and strength to hang in there and keep on believing, keep on dreaming; in short to just keep on keeping on.

I've often studied crowds on city streets thinking, 'What are they all striving for? Have they definite goals for which they are working and will those goals bring them happiness and satisfaction?' It is all very well to be an achiever if what you have achieved brings you happiness and a sense of having done something of value. But is the individual who finds only unhappiness at the end of all his efforts really an achiever? For example, was the notable actress I once

Consciously compete with only one person —
yourself.
Always try to get ahead of yourself, perfecting your skills to do better and even better.

met who had achieved fame and lots of money really a valid achiever?

At a party in Hollywood I met this famous star and had a short but unforgettable conversation with her. She was very beautiful and sophisticated and naturally she was accepted as a superachiever. A sparkling group of lesser stars hovered around her. She was laughing, sprightly, and witty.

Finally, she came over to me and said she was glad to see me. I said I was glad to see her too and added, 'You act happy.' She replied, 'You're right, it is an act. I'm not happy. Actually, I've never had a dozen happy days in my life. And I would like to be happy, but I guess it's just not for me.'

'Well,' I said, 'at least you've got it over Napoleon.'

'What's Napoleon got to do with it?' she asked in surprise. 'You say you've never had a dozen happy days in your life. When Napoleon was on Saint Helena he said that he had had no more than six happy days in his life. You're way ahead of him.'

'So,' I asked, 'your great achievements have not brought you happiness?'

'No, but I know how to be happy without your reminding me. I was brought up in the same faith as you were. I know the way to happiness but in trying to be top dog I've neglected it.' And to my surprise she said, 'Thanks for reminding me. I'll try to start doing the things I know so well.' As we separated, I thought of the statement in the Bible, 'These things have I spoken unto you, that my joy might remain in you, and that your joy might be full.'

A famous psychiatrist said that the chief duty of a human being is to endure life. I think the chief

176

duty of a human being is to overcome life, to master it, and thereby find happiness. But how many people really are happy?

I read in a newspaper about a Kiwanis Club whose members tried to give away one hundred one-dollar bills. On the streets of the city, where crowds were the thickest, they gave every person who looked genuinely happy a one-dollar bill. How many bills do you think they handed out? Twenty-two! Can it be that only twenty-two people out of the great throng were happy?

People of an artless nature seem to find happiness. By artless I mean people who are childlike in their mental attitudes, who are great enough to think childlike thoughts. A child has a sense of wonder and perceptiveness that brings happiness.

I was staying one night with an old friend whose home is amidst the pine woods of southern Georgia. I awakened in the morning and was sitting quietly when all of a sudden the song of a mockingbird burst in on me. The bird was right outside my window in a tree, singing at the top of its voice. It was beautiful. Soaring, cascading, lilting notes ascended from this bird to the God who made it.

I sat listening to the mockingbird, thinking, 'It hasn't anything to worry about, doesn't have to pay taxes. It doesn't have to worry about what goes on in Washington or city hall. It's just happy.' Then I heard another voice, the voice of an old man, singing an old gospel hymn, 'O Happy Day.' I caught the words, 'O happy day that fixed my choice . . . when Jesus washed my sins away.' I called out the window to the old man, 'You're happy, aren't you?'

He said, 'Yes, sir. I come out here every morning to do the yard work and I sing along with the birds.'

'Is that bird here every morning?' I asked.

'Every morning,' he said, 'and every morning I sing too.'

I asked, 'Is the mockingbird singing 'O Happy Day' too?'

'Yes, sir, in its own language that's exactly what it's singing. You see we're both God's creatures. The bird sits on a bough and has feathers, and I stand on the ground with gray hair on my head, but we're both singing the same song of happiness!'

As we have been saying, those persons who do the most creative things in their work, whatever it is, are the exciting top performers of this world, and excellence marks their achievements.

One day, in mid-morning, my brother Leonard and I were driving to the Tampa airport. As we approached a village, Leonard said, 'There is a restaurant here that is always crowded. You see, it's famous for its pies. They're absolutely super. The lady who bakes them is top-performer number one in the pie business in my book.'

I glanced at my watch. 'It's only ten-fifteen and we had a pretty hefty breakfast. It's too early for lunch.' Then I weakened. 'Tell you what. In the interests of research for the book I'm writing, even if it is only ten-fifteen, let's stop and get a piece of that pie.' I was impressed by the alacrity with which Leonard agreed.

We both ordered cherry pie in the rather plain restaurant, which was already well filled. The pie came. It was delicious; big red cherries, the juice deliciously oozing out and the crust crisply melting in your mouth.

'You know something,' I said, 'this has to be the best pie in the world, but to be sure this one piece is truly representative, don't you think we should sample another one?'

Leonard, always cooperative, agreed and we ordered apple pie this time; and if possible, it was even better than the cherry. After consuming this one I said enthusiastically, 'I've just got to meet the lady who makes these pies and shake her by the hand.' I made this request to the waitress. 'Sure,' she said. 'She's right out there in the kitchen. Go ahead.'

In the kitchen I found several women. All were dressed in blue smocks save a middle-aged woman who had on an immaculate white outfit. 'Ma'am, did you bake those pies we just ate?'

She must have been a transplanted Yankee, for she was really closemouthed. 'Who else?' she replied.

'Well, ma'am, I want to tell you that I have eaten pies all over the world. And I grew up in Ohio where they have the best cooks and bakers in the world, but I've got to admit that I never really had pie that is pie until now. Yours is by all odds the best pie I ever did eat.'

To which she only said, 'That's what they all say.'

'And may I ask how many pies do you make every day?'

'I make forty-seven.'

'And do you enjoy making pies?'

'What do you think? I wouldn't do it if didn't.' And she added, 'It's the way I serve.'

Having finished this, for her, long speech she clammed up. As Leonard and I resumed our journey, I said, 'Do you know something? I've just met one of the most top performers I've ever encountered.'

179

'How do you rate this woman to be that?' asked Leonard.

'Well, she loves what she is doing. She doesn't tire of getting up early six days a week to bake forty-seven pies. She has the highest standards of quality and workmanship. She isn't boastful, just takes praise in stride. Obviously she loves God, goes to her church on Sunday, and bakes pies not to rake in money, but to serve. So in my opinion she has in her nature that extra something that makes her a top performer, maybe number one in her specialty. In her own way she is just as surely a top performer as the most publicized big-time operation, for she is a person of excellence in what she does.'

So I philosophized as we drove along. Leonard concurred, 'Anyone who does her work with the skill this woman shows certainly has that extra something God puts into human nature, and she has it pretty fully.'

And he added, 'Another sure thing—we're not going to need any lunch today.'

How does one become a top performer? A predominant factor I have observed in top performers is simply that they try and keep on trying. They try to do their best. They do not try to be rich or famous or impress anyone. And they consciously compete with only one person—themselves. They are not out to get ahead of anyone else. But they are always trying to get ahead of themselves by perfecting their skills so as to do better and even better.

The famous artist Eric Sloane was my friend. He lived just up the road a few miles from my farm in Dutchess County, New York. He was a rare genius of a man who made much of his life from humble beginnings, because he took the talent given to him and stepped it up by always working and trying to exceed his previous efforts.

He painted rural scenes like old red barns in New York State and Vermont; a haystack in a field, a churn by a milk house. He painted a picture for me, which I cherish and which hangs in my library. It's of a white-steepled church in a small village in autumn. In the foreground is a rambling stone wall. Early in life his paintings sold for very little; later they became collectors' items—costly too.

He was one of our greatest painters of the sky above, which Emerson called the daily bread of the soul. He made a lifelong study of the sky, its coloring, changing aspects, its cloud formations. His sky pictures were masterpieces, not only of beauty, but of profound thoughtfulness as well.

So he added to the total of American art. Then came the day when he laid down his palette and brushes and quietly went home to God leaving behind the beauty he created.

I conducted his funeral in a little Connecticut town one spring afternoon. His ashes were placed under a gigantic boulder in the garden of the museum honouring him. In the huge rock is carved his name, Eric Sloane, and a statement he often made: 'God knows I tried.' If God knows that you and I try, He will come to our aid with additional support.

While working on this chapter I was seated in the Admirals Club of American Airlines at La Guardia Airport waiting for my plane. Looking around, it seemed that the proportion of glum faces was greater than usual. This atmosphere of gloom served as a contrasting background for a man who hobbled in on crutches. His neck was also encased in bandages. But he was laughing and exchanging wisecracks with associates. On the way out he spoke to me and I commented, 'Your cheerfulness helps make my day.'

A shadow of pain crossed his face. 'I'm trying,' he responded, 'and believe me, trying helps. God bless you.' And he went through the exit, leaving an upbeat spirit in his wake. In a land of top performers it is a pretty well-known fact that faith in God is an important factor in achievement, for faith keeps people trying and ultimately reaching their goals.

There is an organization known as the Horatio Alger Association of Distinguished Americans. The members are men and women who started in humble circumstances and through consistent effort became outstanding leaders in industry and other areas. I have attended some of the dinners of this organization at which the award winners said a few words. It was noticeable that the awardees always credited their success to the fact that they tried and kept trying and to their faith in God, who helped them along the way, especially in those times when the going got really hard.

The success potential, another name for the ability to do what you are doing with skill and excellence, is, I believe, inherent in every normally intelligent person. If this is true, why then do some persons become top performers and others do not? Motivation or the lack of it seems the most accurate answer to that question. Motivation makes a person believe that he can do things. It causes him to know he can meet and overcome all adversities in the process. And it keeps him going, working, striving, thinking, believing, and forever trying all the way in all the vicissitudes of his career.

I was talking along this line one noonday at the weekly luncheon meeting of the Central Rotary Club in Hong Kong. Afterward a Chinese man, a member of the club, said, 'You are so right in what you said in your speech today.' He then related his own personal story. It seems that years before, as a young man, he and his wife and two young children lived in Shanghai. The Communists took over the government, and confiscation of property left this formerly fairly prosperous family practically destitute. 'Some inner urge,' he continued, 'caused us to leave our home with only the clothes on our backs and a few extra things we could carry. I remember that I looked around our home and could take only my Bible which I put under my shirt. Then we started walking. We slept at night in open country. We walked to Hong Kong and slipped across the border.'

'There we found thousands of displaced, freedom-loving Chinese like ourselves. Like them we found old boxes and pieces of tin and put up a rude shelter. We were fed at soup kitchens provided by the Hong Kong government, standing in long lines at meal times to get our rations.

'To keep up my spirit I constantly read my Bible and prayed to God. He gave me the feeling that I could take better care of my family, that we could rise above this existence, that in fact I could actually be somebody sometime. So I never lost faith. We held on month after month. God seemed to tell me to encourage our neighbors, so we talked to them about faith and belief.

'Then one day reading the blessed Scriptures I came to Philippians 4:13, 'I can do all things through Christ which strengtheneth me.' Now sir,' he said with a look of wonder, 'I had read that a thousand times but this time it came to me that action was now demanded of me. Then I began to think, really think, and God opened up little opportunities. Wonderful little things happened. Result! Over the years I became a businessman in this city. God has prospered me and always I have worked upon that formula God gave me.'

I count that brief meeting with that Chinese man as one of the motivational events of my life. For he gave me in that conversation a priceless formula. I've lived by it ever since. I earnestly commend it to you. It will work for anyone who believes it and works with it. Don't brush it off, for this formula is a pearl of great price.

Prosperity and success did not come easily to our Chinese friend. He had to try and try and keep on trying. The going was tough and rugged all the way, but he stuck it out. He never lost heart. He never quit. He continued to believe, to study, to work, to try and try again. He was a positive thinker who never let negatives take hold. He was a man of faith forever. And finally he became a winner. Indeed he became a top performer of excellence.

And what are these stories of achievers meant to do for you and for me? Simply to remind us that with the Plus Factor working and the Lord helping us, we too can achieve our goals.

16

The Plus Factor of Good Health

*P*eople today are health-conscious as never before. Newspapers, magazines, radio, and TV feature the subject prominently. Our office receives thousands of communications in the course of a year, as people write to us about their problems. And the number-one problem in the majority of these letters is health, either that of the writer or the health of a loved one.

How does a non-medical writer go about giving suggestions for having and keeping good health? Obviously, if the writer himself has good health he can share personal information as to the measures he takes toward achieving it. In as much as my wife, Ruth, and I have always worked together as a team, I'm going to share a double secret and outline how we both have maintained well-being and energy.

Our life-style is that of a working couple. For example, we are the executives of two rather large magazine publishing organizations. Ruth edits my books and is also an author in her own right. She travels with me to my many speaking engagements. On such trips we work together on manuscripts and a large volume of mail. Our schedule requires that we be healthy, for energy is needed and only out of health can energy be derived and maintained.

Ruth has had good health all her life. And so have I. We have been married for over fifty years, and I have learned to regard her as a repository of wisdom and insight. I asked her, 'Why have we always been blessed with good health? I am writing this book to help people, so let's give our joint formula for being healthy.'

The following are some principles of good health as we have found them in our own experience.

First of all we have found that one way to be healthy and also happy is to have interesting work to do. We are healthy, vigorous, energetic, and yet we work hard every day and have followed this busy routine for years. We have breakfast before 7 A.M. and work at home on papers and manuscripts until 8:30 or 9:00, then go to the office. There we follow a busy schedule of meetings, conferences, interviews, dictation of mail, and telephone calls. Lunch consists of half a sandwich and half an apple at our desks and uses up about fifteen minutes.

When we are not at Guideposts or the Foundation for Christian Living, we have a heavy travel schedule of speaking engagements before national business conventions throughout the United States and Canada and occasionally in countries as far away as New Zealand and Australia. We like this life so much that we take very few vacation periods. And this busy schedule is followed month after month and year after year. Despite it all, or perhaps because of our intense interest in these activities, we are healthy.

Actually we seldom think of our taken-for-granted well-being except when it comes to writing a chapter of this sort. Then we stop to ask each other why and how in such busy lives we have been able to preserve strength and energy over so many intensely active years. We are not geniuses, just plain everyday people; and the fact that we can continue to be extremely active, going from one business to another, traveling 150,000 miles a year on speaking engagements and still be in the best of health means that others can do the same. If you will think right, pray, and keep relaxed, you will go a long way toward well-being.

Let's discuss eating, which I feel is basic to health. We eat simply. A bowl of cereal with a banana and a piece of toast or English muffin for breakfast, a meager lunch at our desk at noon as previously described, and an early dinner consisting of fish or chicken with vegetables and a salad. If we have meat, it is probably veal. We don't count calories, but we are sparing of sweets, never have a saltshaker or sugar bowl on the table, and keep the total food intake under control. We never take snacks between meals.

We go to bed early when we have no engagements that keep us out late. Before going to bed or before dinner, or both times when we are at the farm, we walk one or two miles and sometimes also swim.

In New York City we walk a mile on Fifth, Madison, or Park Avenue daily. We have a couple of favorite restaurants, one Chinese, the other German, each a mile away, and we walk there and back. Top priority is given to walking, which we believe does much to maintain top condition.

As previously stated, we do not believe work hurts, but rather helps, for if you are deeply and intensely interested in work, it frees you from many ills. We haven't time to be unhealthy. The Lord knows that and generously cooperates by keeping both of us fit to do the work to which He has called us. Our Plus Factors are thus kept in good working order, constantly producing the energy to keep going and handle our considerable responsibilities.

But when at the start of writing this chapter I put the question to Ruth, 'Why are we in good health at my age and yours?' she replied, 'Well, for one thing we are not people who worry or have fears and we don't hate anyone. And we love God and the Lord Jesus and people and we truly try to do the Lord's will. And that's about it,' she concluded.

'Think Positive, Stay Healthy' was the headline over an article in the *Sunday Times* of London on July 27, 1986. The article declares that 'depression and anxiety undermine the body's ability to fend off diseases.'

The popular belief that illness is more likely to follow anxiety and depression has recently been substantiated by scientific studies. Immunologists are discovering more about the link between mind and body.

For instance, we know that during stressful periods the body produces large amounts of a steroid called cortisol. This inhibits the work of macrophage cells which are a key part of our immune system. This means the body can no longer respond normally to infection.

Researchers, having evidence that stress depresses the immune system, now will try to find out what sort of events enhance the immune system. . . .

Dr. [Stephen] Greer of the Royal Marsden Hospital has shown how these worries can also affect the patient's physical condition. He looked at the mental attitudes of women who had a breast removed as part of cancer treatment and found that those who had a positive attitude were twice as likely to survive for 10 years as those who were depressed.

'We will be teaching patients cognitive strategies—that is to say, mental tricks to challenge their negative thinking,' he explains.

These and other significant findings being widely reported today substantiate the presence of good health assets in the mind and in our attitudes. This extra supportive power that we call the Plus Factor is a spiritual faculty given to each of us by the Creator to keep us in shape mentally and physically. It only makes sense that God wants those marvelous instruments which He made, mind and body, to work as well as He designed them to.

Having worked closely with people and their problems over many years, I have no hesitancy whatsoever in asserting that in my opinion and experience one secret of good health is to have soul or spirit health. To live by the teachings and spirit of Jesus Christ is to be healthy mentally, and mental health leads to wholeness of the total personality. I do not mean that religious people don't get sick, for, of course, they do. But it is a demonstrated fact that religious faith generally speaking has a positive effect on health, and departure from morality, a negative effect.

It is perhaps strange how inner confusion, even deterioration, is often caused by guilt feelings. We are living in a time when some people actually pretend to believe it's okay to engage in wrongful acts as long as it's their own business or doesn't hurt anyone. Well, the trouble is it does hurt someone—you! Wrongdoing eats at your well-being. It can actually affect the body and mind adversely and often causes ill health.

An outstanding ear physician tells me that trouble with the ear—such as roaring in the ear, muffled hearing, imbalance, dizziness—doesn't always result from a physical problem. It can be caused by guilt feelings.

Recently this distinguished doctor, a leading man in his speciality in the state, told of a patient, a woman, who complained of pain in her left ear. He examined her carefully and could find nothing wrong. She came back several times and said, 'Doctor, there's got to be something wrong with my ear.'

The doctor said, 'Look, I've been over your ear completely and find nothing amiss.'

He studied her intently. She was obese, very heavy for her age and height. He thought she would have been handsome had she not been so heavy. Obviously she was a compulsive eater. There are compulsive drinkers and there are compulsive eaters, and both are driven by inherent emotional conflict. When you see a person drinking or eating heavily, excessively so, you can pretty well figure that he or she is troubled mentally or emotionally. People who overeat are often trying to eat away something that is eating at them.

The doctor asked the patient why she allowed herself to become so heavy. 'I guess it's because I'm so unhappy,' she lamented. 'I was married and was unfaithful to my husband. We got a divorce. Now I've been having an affair with a married man. But what does that have to do with my ear or my eating?'

'It could have everything to do with your ear, and your eating too,' said the doctor.

'Okay!' she exclaimed, 'what can I do? I admit that I'm really quite miserable and I know what I'm doing is wrong, but how can I help myself?'

The doctor replied, 'First, we've got to get rid of your guilt feelings. It's doubtful that you will ever be really happy or physically well until you deal with your inner conflicts and get them resolved. So we'd better drain your mind of those guilt feelings.'

When she finally came to grips with her guilt feelings, she stopped seeing the married man. Gradually her weight was reduced by thirty pounds. She became a healthy, happy woman and had real peace of mind. Then her ear trouble cleared up.

Guilt feelings can cause trouble mentally and even physically in many ways. Sometimes people are troubled by anxiety and fear due to long-held guilt. Indeed, guilt and fear are so inextricably interlocked that when these two enemies of human well-being gang up they can make life quite miserable. Anyone who suffers from fear or anxiety needs to face honestly the possibility that guilt may be involved. Its elimination is a necessity for healing.

A man I knew became a victim of anxiety in a dramatic reversal of personality, a personality which formerly was free of abnormal fear. It came out that he had developed an enormous sense of guilt based on violation of his moral code. Sadly he discovered that these basic and deeply ingrained convictions could not so easily be set aside without disastrous disintegration of personality.

I recommended several steps designed to bring peace and renewal. First, to stop what he was doing. Second, a complete mental catharsis under the guidance of a competent spiritual counselor. By that I meant he was to empty out all the evil he had thought and done, holding nothing back. A good washing out of the mind can do wonders for anyone. Third, he was to ask and receive divine forgiveness. Forgiveness is quickly and generously given the sincere person. Fourth, he was to forgive himself, which is even more difficult. And no longer was he to condemn himself. The ego instinctively believes it must continually punish and repunish itself. Self-forgiveness is vital, for it turns off abnormal self-punishment. Fifth, he was to rebuild his personality on a moral basis harmonious with his deepest convictions.

When the man followed this prescription, he found peace of mind once again, and good health too.

We are dealing here with the prevention of ill health rather than the curing of disease. I think it is an indisputable fact that the person who develops and maintains a wholesome, healthy-minded spiritual life pattern will be most likely to preserve strength and energy and a state of wellness. That person will be free of what we may call the 'virus' of resentment—'Sick' thoughts will not be able to undermine health.

However, that there can be a healing level where spiritual forces also operate with curative effect seems indicated by the experiences of many perfectly reliable persons. A friend sent me a clipping from *The Daily Review* of Towanda, Pennsylvania, dated August 18, 1985. It carries the story of the healing of Sally Schultz,

Think positive.
Stay healthy.

a mother and highly respected nurse in that community. I do not know Sally Schultz, or have any information about her case beyond the news story by Wes Skillings. But I do find this story of healing strangely moving and also indicative of the operation of the Plus Factor.

There's an ageless quality about Sally Schultz. She's one of those rare people who seems to have reversed the cycle that steadily robs us of youth and vitality. Her rust-hued hair and delicate porcelain skin, highlighted by roseate cheeks that would put the finest rouge to shame, make one forget that this woman is the mother of three children in their twenties.

It wasn't always that way. She was suffering from a disease that had turned sunshine into an enemy. When she was outside, even in summer, she was wrapped in a cocoon of long sleeves, pants, gloves, hats, and scarfs.

The bottom line was the sun would kill her.

This was a disease called lupus. After an automobile accident 20 years ago, it suddenly came into her life. The accident broke her jaw and cracked and jammed bones and tendons in her neck. She became afflicted with a battery of problems that caused her body to deteriorate. Pain became her closest companion. Among the most brutal invaders was arthritis that made the simplest movements agony and kept her from sleeping for several nights at a time. She was allergic to everything, particularly aspirin—and it seemed as if all the advances in modern medicine were useless in her case.

Sally started searching for answers. The more she read, the more she became convinced that the power to conquer her afflictions was within her. Though she was not brought up in a religious household, she found tremendous relief in the power of prayer and meditation. In her readings she kept finding one key—the answer is in your head, in some corner of the brain or waiting to be tapped in the subconscious. If that were true, and she knew innately that it was, she wondered if the illnesses themselves, all feeding upon each other, had grown from the seeds sprouted by negative forces somewhere within her consciousness.

'If it's in my head, tell me and I'll accept it,' she told the doctors. But, of course, all the physical evidence was there—in the tests and her growing medical records. The more she read, the more she became convinced that there was power within her that could defeat these invaders. Most important, like all believers in prayer, she believed in miracles.

A miracle came for Sally Schultz in the early morning hours. She had been unable to sleep. She dozed off briefly, awakening with a tremendous urge to get out of bed. There was no pain. She got up and walked. No pain. Sat down. Stood up. All the movements that had been so unbearable were now effortless, painless.

It never came back. She was cured somehow. To her the years that have passed since have been years of constant healing. 'I've actually gone to a higher plane of healing,' she says.

'It's mind, body, and soul,' she says quietly. A strong proponent of natural foods, vitamins, and herbs, she is probably best known locally as the proprietor of a local health food store.

'But you need spiritual food too,' she says. 'None of it can happen unless the ego goes out the door.'

She is certain that there is a constant battle between positive and negative energies, on another plane.

'I believe there is an open channel to the Creator,' she continues. 'He is our past, present, and future.' It's a channel into which we can all tap in, she says. 'You have to lose you to find Him,' is her simple assessment.

As a person who believes in visions and directives from a higher realm, she often feels called to a certain passage in the Bible and has frequently awakened in the middle of the night, suddenly aware of someone else's need for prayer or support. She says these directives have yet to be wrong.

Although lupus is a disease known for its unpredictability, with flare ups and remissions appearing at any time, there is reason to believe that the victim's mental outlook plays a role in its course.

In this case Mrs. Schultz became convinced that a power within her was working to restore health. It would seem that we can identify the power to which she referred as the Plus Factor, that extra something that the Creator placed within us for our benefit.

My brother Dr. Robert Clifford Peale was a physician and surgeon, a graduate of Harvard Medical School. I always thought that he was truly a natural-born doctor. He was generously endowed with a loving attitude and his patients were devoted to him. He told me once, 'Norman, you will live a long time even though you drive yourself with work.' Asked why he thought so, he replied, 'You have learned the priceless secret of having inner peace amidst outward turmoil. And,' he added, 'Ruth has the same gift, more so than you.

If Bob was right in his diagnosis it is because Ruth and I have been fortunate to find one of the greatest blessings in this world, which the Scriptures refer to as 'the peace of God which passes all understanding.' You can have it also.

As I write these lines, I am working in my room in Switzerland looking out on a blue lake surrounded by snowcapped mountains. The blue sky overhead is dotted by a few fleecy white clouds. This fabulous spot contains the peace of the world in full measure.

Just a moment ago nature put on one of its most spectacular demonstrations. The widest rainbow I have ever seen stretched from the lake over a high snow-clad mountain to touch down in a deep valley in the Alps. There was about this gigantic rainbow a deep benediction of peace and hope. But as ineffable as nature is in the effect of natural beauty on the mind, it cannot match the peace of God in its healing effect on the human mind. Jesus refers to this comparison, 'Peace I give unto you: not as the world giveth, give I unto you' (John 14:27). It cannot be stated too strongly that God-inspired inner peace produces harmony and well-being mentally and physically and is thereby the greatest boon to health.

According to a report in the International Journal of Cardiology (January 1986), religious belief may be protective against heart disease. This was the conclusion of Israeli researchers who found lower heart-attack rates among devout, Orthodox Jews than among non-practicing Jews. In this study of 500 men and women the researchers cited psychological and social factors as playing possible roles, but said: 'The strong belief in a supreme being and the role of prayer may in themselves be protective.'

My friend and physician Dr. John C. Carson of La Jolla, California, is always kind enough to give me a physical examination when he spends a month each summer as the doctor at Lake Mohonk, which is situated in several thousand acres of ancient forestation in New York State. John runs daily amidst this quietness and has transmitted to me the sense of peace he has obviously derived from this environment. In a lesser circumference on our farm not far distant, in walking among the trees and meadows, I have found an inner peace that has been reflected in normal blood pressure readings and in good heart action.

That thinking can affect health both for good or ill has often been demonstrated. The late James A. Farley, onetime postmaster general, was a friend of mine. One day when I encountered him on the street and stopped to chat, I noticed once again his vigorous health. I knew that he was over eighty at the time and admiringly said, 'Jim, you actually look the same as you did twenty-five years ago. How come you look so healthy and show no signs of getting old?' He smiled and said, 'I never think any old thoughts.'

What are old thoughts? Perhaps they axe threadbare, worn-out, tired thoughts about life, its cares and troubles as faced by us all. Old thoughts sometimes take the form of resentment, even hatred. If sustained over time, such thinking can produce ill effects physically. Explosive anger has well-known reactions. When anger is perhaps less than heated but seethes constantly, insidious harmful effects can result and in time become acute.

Some people on the other hand constantly infuse their thought processes with the zest, the opportunity, and even the wonder of living. They do not sag and lose their mental and spiritual verve. The Plus Factor is constantly going for them keeping them alive, vital, interested.

It is important to expect good health, for that which is imaged and expected tends to become fact. A few times in my own life I have experienced a crisis in health that caused some concern. But even in such emergency I always expected that the end result would be good. And, in every instance I have emerged in excellent condition. Positive imaging and expectation of good health, I believe, do much to activate a positive response in mind and body. The Plus Factor constantly tries to produce the health status that is imaged positively. Spiritual power gives impetus to the Plus Factor.

This spiritual power, which, I believe, transcends physical force, will not work, nor could it be expected to do so, when it is accompanied by practices that run counter to health. Positive thinking, positive imaging, and positive expectation with all their creativity can be frustrated by a life-style that flouts the laws of well-being. But when one lives sensibly, thinks positively, and believes in the best outcomes, good health, while not guaranteed, is more likely to be achieved and maintained. (Of course, professional medical help is needed, and you should let your doctor help you maintain good health.)

To sum up, here are the simple good-health rules that Ruth and I practice:

Rules for Good Health and Positive Living

1. Have interesting work to do. Keep active at something worthwhile.
2. Eat simply. Keep your food intake under control.
3. Go to bed early and get up early.
4. Give top priority to walking every day. Swimming is also helpful.
5. Love God, don't hate anyone, and don't be afraid.
6. Never let a sense of guilt fester in you. Get it cleaned.
7. Develop spirit and soul health.
8. Cultivate the 'peace of God that passes understanding.'
9. Expect and image good health.
10. Through spiritual cultivation keep your Plus Factor robust.

17

Turn Setbacks Into Comebacks

Jim Decker's name kept coming to mind. And this was a bit strange, for I hadn't seen him lately. But I have learned that when a person continues to come up in my thoughts, it may mean that I'd better do something about it. And I'm usually glad I did.

I went to see Jim and found him slumped in his office chair the picture of gloom and despair. 'What's wrong, Jim?' I asked. 'Usually you're right up there on top, happy and positive. Why the gloom? You could cut it with a knife.'

'Norman, I've had the biggest setback of my business career,' he said dolefully. 'I've lost my best account, a third of my business. Now I know you'll give me some of that positive-thinking stuff of yours. But I'm afraid it won't work this time. This one's knocked me for a loop. It's a terrible setback.'

'Do you want to tell me about it?' I asked, adding, 'I'm no wise man, but sometimes it helps just to talk to someone, especially a friend who thinks you are a great guy, who loves you, who believes in you.'

'Yeah,' he said, 'and it's mighty good of you to come. It's just like you. You're so right. I've been thinking and thinking until I'm getting more and more confused. Maybe it will help to talk it out. How much talk can you take? How much are you good for?'

'When I have to go, Jim, I'll let you know. Start talking.' And he did. He laid it all out, condemning himself for 'dumb' actions, stupid mistakes, but gradually his talk turned from what he should have done to what he might do, to what he could do. He began to explore solutions. Mentally turning from the past he started facing the future. And that was just the beginning.

When a big setback hits you, the first step on the road to recovery is to start turning from the past and look toward the future. This didn't happen all at once with Jim, however. I entered that office at 3 P.M. and finally left at 5:45 P.M. I listened to over two hours of talk.

And I am glad I did, for by talking it out to a caring friend Jim Decker worked his way past that setback and ultimately wove it into his experience creatively.

Here's how he got the solution for that recovery. Along about two hours after he started talking I interrupted: 'Excuse me, Jim, do you ever read *Guideposts*?'

'*Guideposts*? Sure I read it. I think it's a terrific magazine. What do you mean do I read *Guideposts*? You know I do.'

'Okay,' I said. 'Then you know the page we call 'Words to Grow On.''

He nodded, 'Good stuff on that page.' He gestured to a pile of *Guideposts* magazines on a table.

202

I hunted through them until I found the September 1986 issue. Then I said, 'Rest your voice and let me read what Grant Teaff, coach of the Baylor University football team, has to say.'

I'm always looking for the right words to encourage my football team. At Baylor University, where I've been head coach for 14 years, I've used everything from praise to provocation to get the best out of my players. But once, the right encouraging words came from a team member.

In 1980 we had a very strong team and had won the first seven games of the season. We were riding high and running a little scared, I think, as the pressure to win increased. Our eighth game was against San Jose State, a team supposedly not up to our caliber.

In a shocking upset San Jose beat us, 30-22. Suddenly our confidence waned. After our loss I kept hearing people say what might have been, shaking their heads over what we could have done. The team seemed to absorb this negative thinking. In the workouts leading up to our next game against the University of Arkansas we couldn't seem to rid ourselves of a lingering defeatist attitude.

Then Kyle Woods came to our dressing room. A year before, Kyle had been injured in a workout that left him paralyzed. He was only a sophomore, a defensive back on the second team, when it happened. Now he would be a cripple for life. This was his first visit to a game in Baylor Stadium since the injury.

Kyle was in the dressing room before the game, in a wheelchair. After our team prayer, I said a few words and then asked Kyle if he had anything to add.

'I sure do,' he said.

I walked over to his wheelchair and pushed him into the center of the room. Kyle paused for a moment and seemed to look every player in the eye. He said, 'Here it is: *You take a setback and you turn it into a comeback.*'

Then Kyle dropped his hands to his side. He had no dexterity in them, but he managed to lock his thumbs around the wheelchair's arms. He pushed downward on the chair with his hands, lifting his body up. With one giant lunge, he stood up.

There he stood in the dressing room, to emphasize the point he'd just made, that 'you can take a setback and turn it into a comeback.' I've never heard a greater message nor seen it so dramatically punctuated.

Then we went out and defeated the University of Arkansas, 42-15, and we went on to become the 1980 Southwest Conference champions.

The Bible says, 'God hath not given us the spirit of fear; but of power, and of love, and of a sound mind'. The Lord wants us to achieve. Out of every setback we can find the comeback He has in mind for us!*

Jim sat nodding his head. Then he got up, walked

---

* Adapted from *Winning: It's How You Play the Game* by Grant Teaff, Word Book, 1985.

around the desk, and put a big hand on my shoulder. 'You know something, Norman! God sent you down here today. That's what I needed to hear. Out of every setback we can find the comeback God has in mind for us.' He went and looked out the window for several minutes. 'Okay, I can make it back now. I know I can. Pray for me and stick with me.'

Fortunately, this was an intelligent and spiritually minded man. He knew the source of power, the way to mount a comeback. He drew on the Plus Factor in his nature. Ultimately, he compensated for this loss of one big account by adding a number of smaller accounts, and so by his own admission was better off in the long run.

Everyone has setbacks. This is a normal fact of life. And when you have more than one in a row, as sometimes happens, it can be very discouraging. If you allow it to be so, it can take the life out of you. But you should always remember that even so, you still have a lot of rebound left. And when you deliberately start calling on your Plus Factor, you can begin the process that turns setbacks into comebacks.

That is what Jim Decker did. How did he do it? Well, I would say he did it because he is a big man, not physically, because he is only average in size. But he is big mentally, big in outlook, big in faith.

Everyone, every man and woman, has something big in him or her, an extraspecial power put there by the Creator Himself. God knew you would have tough times—when things would go wrong, when everything would seem to be against you. The Creator was aware that setbacks would come and you would be discouraged and feel defeated or that crises would suddenly develop and you wouldn't think you could handle them. He knew that sometime, somewhere along the line, maybe more than once in life, you would be in sore need of extra strength. So He provided a mechanism to produce this power and built it into your mind and body—and it works miraculously, it's one of the wonders that you possess. It is the Plus Factor.

As a matter of fact, God Almighty made you much bigger than you have ever thought you are. Perhaps you write yourself off, put yourself down as just an average person not able to take much trouble or bear up under the vicissitudes of life. 'It's all more than I can take,' we say despondently. But when we start growing big spiritually, then we grow big mentally and big, too, in faith—faith in God and also faith in ourselves.

A man once told me he read in one of my books about praying big, believing big, thinking big. He admitted he had thought himself small. So he started to pray big, believe big, and think big. After a while he began to grow big. He developed a bigger faith, bigger thought power, a bigger personality. 'I adopted the Twelve Big Plan,' he told me. Twelve ways to grow bigger within yourself. Here is the plan he gave me: 'Pray big, think big, believe big, act big, dream big, work big, give big, forgive big, laugh big, image big, love big, live big.' Carry that list with you daily, look at it often and you will take on an inner bigness such as you've never had.

You and I, and indeed everyone, have lodged within an indomitable, superstrong quality. It can be summoned to our assistance in times of emergency. Physically it is often called 'a shot of adrenaline.' It results in a sudden access of strength that dramatically supplements normal energy. This may be regarded as a demonstration of the basic Plus Factor.

A man five feet nine inches in height and weighing only 148 pounds was driving behind a huge tractor-trailer. Suddenly the truck swerved, jackknifed, and crashed into a ditch where it turned over. Gasoline spilling out ignited and fire was already spreading over the truck when the driver of the car jammed on his brakes, jumped out, and ran to the cab. He found the driver slumped over the wheel in shock and pinned by the warped doom. He tried the door, but it had been badly jammed in the accident. He tried again mustering what seemed all his strength, but the door would not budge.

The fire now roaring through the length of the vehicle made him terrifyingly aware of the immediate possibility of explosion. He had to get the driver out of there and fast. 'Oh, God, help me. Give me strength,' he cried. He grabbed the cab door once again and, summoning additional strength, jerked the door open, grabbed the stunned driver, and pulled him out just in time. Where did this extra strength come from? Where else but from the inner Plus Factor called into action by a life or death crisis. What he did not have the strength to do under normal circumstances, he found he did have when desperate circumstances required it.

When a setback hits you, immediately get up, look in a mirror, and tell yourself, 'I am bigger than I think I am. I have the great God helping me.' Then draw on that big something within called the Plus Factor. You will be strong enough to turn that setback into a comeback.

My friend Smith Johnson is a remarkable man, an ingenious engineer, builder of a successful rubber company, an artist, and a man of positive action. He stood up to fear in his childhood and as a result became bigger than fear. And that is being big, for fear can be very big indeed. Mr. Johnson says, 'I am reminded of an incident which happened in my youth when I was about ten years old. I had always been frightened of thunder and lightning to the extent that sometimes I crawled under the bed during heavy storms. It was on such a night about ten o'clock that I made a momentous decision. I would go outdoors and face the elements, whatever the consequences. I left my room, where I had gone to bed, and dressed with overshoes and raincoat, crept downstairs and outside without rousing my parents. Our house was out in the country a mile or so from town. Back of our house was a ten-acre lot and then another ten acres of woods. I made my way across the lot with the lightning blazing and the thunder cracking in my ears. Across the lot I went and into the woods where the only light I had to make my way was the lightning which flashed almost continually. Stumbling over logs and through the thick underbrush I finally reached the back fence which was a half-mile from our house. The storm, if possible, had become worse, and I sat on the top rail of the fence. The rain pelted me and a strong wind tried to take my coat off, but I had a wonderful inside feeling of accomplishment. I had braved the storm and was still alive. Then I retraced my steps back home and it didn't seem half so far. I crept up to my room without waking my parents. I slept the sleep of the happy, even going to sleep before the storm stopped.

'The next test to which I put myself was overcoming the fear of a building on my way through a park to

*To every
disadvantage
there is a
corresponding
advantage.*

school. This was called the pavilion because many years before they had held dances in it. It was boarded up and generally shunned by the townspeople because it was said to be haunted. I was so terrified by it that I usually ran past as far from it as possible. But one evening with my newfound courage I took this shortcut home instead of going by the road, which was farther. I went boldly around the building looking for a way to get into it. By good fortune I found a loose board, which I removed. Through this opening I forced my skinny body. It was indeed spooky as I walked across the creaky floor from one end to the other. I even explored the long unused kitchen, which was particularly dark and to my wrought-up imagination very hazardous. Again I felt that sweet feeling of accomplishment as I stood my ground in the deserted building.

'I feel that these two experiences had a great and profound effect on my life which is drawing to a close at eighty-eight years. Was it God who gave me the strength to do these two simple things, but most important to me? I don't know. But my faith in God and myself, I believe, have helped me during a life when there were many narrow escapes from disaster or death. And I am most thankful for it.'

The fact is that we *can* handle and rise above things much better than we think. Yet, sometimes mere common everyday difficulties that we all have can add up and eventually defeat us if we allow them to do so. A lady wrote me from Florida. 'About sixty years ago I had trouble getting to sleep. My mother told our minister about it because she figured a twelve-year-old should not have that trouble.

'The pastor took me aside and said he heard I had a problem with insomnia. He then took a piece of paper and printed eight words: quietly, restfully, easily, patiently, peacefully, trustfully, serenely, joyously. He handed it to me and said, 'Repeat these words slowly and think of the meaning of each one. By the time you reach the end, I am sure you will have dozed off.'

'I still have it in my Bible and when a restless night comes I repeat the words and think of that kind, understanding minister.'

As a twelve-year-old girl this woman found a technique that worked on the problem of sleeplessness and years later, when she had become elderly, it was still working. I've believed and taught in books and speeches that there is a workable formula for every trouble. It's like finding a cure for a disease: Discovery goes on constantly. There is a way to attack every setback and it is often some simple, tried and true method.

My mother often said, 'Whenever a door shuts, it means that God has an open door for you down the way.' She believed this, for it operated again and again in the life of my parents. So she taught it to her children, my brothers and myself; and the three of us believed it, having seen it work for Mother and Father. Our firm belief in it proved effective for us as well. We were not much upset with setbacks for we believed that a comeback was just waiting down the road a piece. And do you know that is exactly the way it worked out for Bob and Leonard and for me and for many to whom we have suggested this principle.

Often a so-called setback is actually a blessing in disguise. Many times setbacks not only lead to comebacks but to even better circumstances than before. 'To every disadvantage there is a corresponding advantage' is a statement often made by W. Clement Stone who has had enough disadvantages to know something about them and what can come of them. By a strong positive attitude and intelligent effort he was able to turn the majority of his setbacks into comebacks. And he says he learned something from each experience. One thing he learned was to look intently into a setback situation for what know-how it might contain, for usually there are some direction signs to that comeback down the road.

A case in which I had some involvement concerned the chief financial officer of a fair-sized investment counseling company. His goal was to succeed to the presidency of the company upon the retirement of the president and chief executive officer. He was sure he would. And why not? He was widely considered to be one of the most knowledgeable men in the investment counseling business.

Yet when the vacancy occurred, he was not selected. Instead a man from a branch office was brought in as president. The bypassed official was, of course, deeply disappointed and angry. He felt that he was unfairly treated and humiliated by this rejection. He loudly declared that the new president 'knows nothing about investment counseling; he is just an ordinary salesman.'

The new president, whom I happened to know quite well, a kindly, thoughtful, Christian man, telephoned me and said he would like to come and talk over a problem with me. The problem was the one I am relating. He told me that it was indeed a fact that the treasurer was the best man in the business—without any question—and he added, 'He has forgotten more about the business than I ever knew. I feel sorry for him, for this is a terrible setback to his career.'

212

'Why then did your board bypass him and select you?' I asked.

Floyd replied, 'It's because he cannot get along with people. He is a genius in finance, but at the same time he's an unapproachable man who just turns people off. The board wanted an administrator who could make decisions and who also liked people and was outgoing and could therefore lead.' He grinned, 'Since he didn't need much ability, they picked on me. But,' he continued, 'I want to help Frank. I won't be in this job all that long at my age, and I'd like to help him recover from this setback and later make a real comeback and succeed me as president.'

'Call on him in his office,' I suggested, 'or better still, go to his home some evening. Let him know how you respect him and his ability and try to help him to change his attitudes toward people. Tell him you're going to have to depend upon him. To change a personality requires delicacy and patience, but you've got both qualities. Later at an appropriate time, if you are sure your board would select him if he changes, you could level with him about the reason he was not promoted.'

Subsequently these two men became good co-workers. The treasurer was completely loyal to his president. Gradually some of the chief executive's affability and caring rubbed off on the other man. At any rate, five years later when Floyd retired, he recommended Frank for the position. Frank was elected by the board and became, so I have been informed, an excellent well-liked administrator. His setback had within it the makeup of his comeback. Fortunately, he was cast in a big mold and did not persist in anger and hostility. He cooperated, he learned about himself, he corrected his weaknesses of personality, and therefore he qualified for a comeback.

I've often thought that Floyd was able to handle this delicate situation so well because for years he had been growing spiritually. His Plus Factor it seemed was working very well indeed.

This is a case where the rebound from a setback to a comeback was engineered by another person. All of which highlights the importance of having friends who know our good points and emphasize them creatively. The more such friends we accumulate, the more we guarantee successful recovery in times of setback. We can build up comeback resources by becoming involved in our communities, always being sensitive to the needs of the other fellow. Not that we do these good deeds to assure a payoff in the form of help for ourselves, but just because it's the right way to live. It is a fact, however, as the Good Book says, if you 'cast your bread upon the water, you will find it after many days.'

When his setback came, Jules Matsoff found that his many friends were the source of his comeback.

When he walked into his clothing store one day in March, he felt about as low as a man can feel. His failing business, Esther's of Hartford, Wisconsin, with aisle after aisle of women's fashions, had been a local institution since 1920. Jules and Roz, his wife of 44 years, had purchased the store from Esther in 1958 and kept the business growing—until now. Now business was shrinking and the outlook was bleak—not the customary outlook for Jules Matsoff.

A talkative, energetic, people-loving, risk-taking businessman, Jules had done an amazing thing for his little town of 7,000 souls. He had made it a magnet for shoppers from the big city. His sales technique was advertising his store heavily on radio and TV stations and in newspapers in Milwaukee, the major metropolitan area 27 miles southeast of Hartford. He even rented the Hartford City Hall every summer and had such a whale of a sale that it drew customers from six counties. A goodly number of retailers in town admit that it was Jules' advertising that brought customers to *their* stores as well.

In 1980 Jules and Roz decided to expand. The Downtown Development Authority was willing to lend them a million dollars at 10 per cent interest to build a mini-mall. Two years later Esther's moved into a modern, red-brick complex with room for nine other stores. Business buzzed. But not for long. No matter how hard he tried, Jules couldn't rent four of the nine stores in the mall. The empty space ate up his profits and he couldn't afford to continue advertising in the Milwaukee media—which sharply curtailed the business generated by city shoppers.

By 1984 newspapers and news stations had noticed that the little mall seemed to have permanent 'For Rent' signs in many windows. Suddenly, 'Financially Troubled' became Esther's first name. Rumors flew that Esther's was on its way out of business. Panicky brides-to-be started calling. 'Mr. Matsoff, I'm getting married in a month! What's going to happen to my wedding gown and bridesmaid dresses?'

Jules assured the young women that their gowns would be delivered on time. But some weren't convinced and canceled their orders. Two top salespeople quit to work in Milwaukee because they believed the business was going under.

In 1986 the Redevelopment Authority had to file a lawsuit demanding the $50,000 the Matsoffs were behind in loan payments. Foreclosure loomed.

Jules' fund of optimism was finally depleted. 'Maybe it's time to call it quits,' he told Roz.

'We can't give up now,' Roz insisted. 'Remember, Esther's even got through the Depression.'

A few months later, Jules found a buyer for the mall. Though his enthusiasm for retailing was at low ebb, Roz persuaded him to look for a new location for Esther's. Half-heartedly, he decided to rent the old closed-up movie theater across the street. Then the Matsoffs did just enough redecorating to make it usable.

Jules continued to worry. 'Roz, we're going to lose too much money when we close the store to make the move. It'll take a week. I've hired five men, but they'll need hundreds of trips to carry everything by hand, out the door, down the sidewalk and across the street!'

Roz stayed calm. 'It'll all work out. What happened to your faith?'

Jules shook his head. 'Maybe God wants us to retire.'

On that March morning of the move, Jules dragged himself downtown, unlocked the door of his beautiful mall store for the last time and heaved a heavy sigh. Just as he flipped on the light switch he noticed a local bakery truck pulling up in front of the store. Two men got out with two huge trays filled with doughnuts and pastries and plopped them down on the jewelry counter.

'Hey, wait a minute. I didn't order that. You must have made a mistake.'

'No mistake, Mr. Matsoff, it's all paid for.'

Before he could call the bakery, another truck from a local restaurant arrived with two 100-cup coffee makers.

Jules did a 180-degree turn. That's when he saw all the people, over a hundred of them, streaming toward the store. His attorney was wearing jeans and a sweatshirt, as were many of the other professional people and business owners. Even Mayor Witt was there in his natty three-piece business suit. Soon they were all chatting, laughing, wolfing down doughnuts and coffee.

'We're here to make the move, Jules. You just tell us what to take first and how to carry it.'

'Hey, ol'buddy,' pinned Dick Furman, manager of the local J.C. Penney store, Esther's biggest competitor, 'We figure you won't have to close the store for a minute. If somebody wants to buy something we're ready to move, we'll just send 'em right up to the cash register!'

Mike LaCrosse, the six-foot-two, 240-pound owner of the Jock Shop, the local sporting-goods store, hollered, 'Hey, Jules, wanna give us a crash course on how to carry these long fancy dresses?'

Jules phoned Roz in the theater store, 'Roz, I don't know what's going on, but there are some crazy people here and they're moving the whole store right now.'

And that's exactly what they did that crisp, sunny March morning in downtown Hartford. Even the police helped direct traffic while Esther's army marched 14,000 items—lock, stock and mannequins—across the street.

They finished the job in just over two hours. Then the movers, en masse marched back inside the empty store and surrounded Jules like players surrounding a coach after the season's most exciting victory. 'Lift him up, guys!' shouted Jim Sarafiny, Jules' attorney.

Using the principles listed here will help you turn your setbacks into comebacks.

From Setbacks to Comebacks

1. Always believe that with God's help you can ultimately turn any setback into a comeback.

2. Picture yourself as having a lot of rebound left in you. Your Plus Factor is still unimpaired.

3. Think positively, especially when you feel the lowest. Remember, in that setback may be the answer to your comeback.

4. Remind yourself that you are bigger than anything that can happen to you.

5. Never be afraid. Stand up to your fear with God. He will give you faith and faith is always bigger and stronger than fear.

6. Pray big, believe big, think big.

7. Always be helpful to others and you will have friends who will help you turn setbacks into comebacks.

Before Jules knew what was happening he was hoisted shoulder high and carried out the door, down the sidewalk, across the street and right into the old theater.

'Hey, Roz, here's the last piece of merchandise. Where do you want us to put it?'

Roz giggled. 'Oh, that's a mark-down. You can toss it in the corner.'

And so it all ended on a happy note. For a certain discouraged small-town retailer had seen a wholesale demonstration of God's Golden Rule.*

Remember always that you can turn setbacks into comebacks with your Plus Factor.

---

* From "Hartford Shows Its Heart" by Patricia Lorenz. Excerpted with permission from *Guideposts* magazine. Copyright © 1986 by Guideposts Associates, Inc., New York.

18

Growing Older With
the Plus Factor

*A*ctress Marie Dressler once said, 'It's not how old you are that matters; it's how you are old.' What a lot of wisdom packed into just thirteen words! We've all known elderly people who seem to pull down the shades and retire from life. They think of themselves as worn out, nonproductive, unattractive, full of health problems. They feel sorry for themselves and expect us to feel sorry for them.

On the other hand, there are older people who sparkle with vitality and the joy of living. They admit cheerfully that they're no longer young, but that doesn't bother them. They think of themselves as wise, experienced, emotionally mature, creative, intellectually alert ... and usually they are. Some mysterious, unseen force keeps them going, sometimes far beyond the allotted biblical span of seventy years.

What is that mysterious unseen force? I think it's yet another manifestation of the Plus Factor.

I am past that biblical span myself, and I think there's a lot to be said for these terrific extra years. The culture we live in tends to put a premium on youth. Our television commercials endlessly extol products supposed to make us look or feel young. The models in our magazine advertisements look as if they had just escaped from the cradle. But aside from an abundance of raw energy, youth is often likely to be lacking in the qualities that make for real happiness: judgment, balance, wisdom, self-control, experience . . . all the values that come as you move along the pathway of life.

It has been my observation that older people are likely to be less self-centered than younger people. They have had time to learn more about loving . . . and living. They are more philosophical about disappointments or setbacks. They are less impatient. They have learned the value of waiting. They are more serene.

In other words, reaching the high plateau of your later years can be a satisfying—even exhilarating— experience, if . . .

If you bring the right attitudes along with you.

One of the key attitudes, certainly, is a strong religious faith. Not long ago a major life insurance company carried out a survey of its policyholders who had lived to be 100 years old ... or more. One of the questions was: What is the most important thing you've learned in your long life? The most frequent answer: Love thy neighbor as thyself.

People who live according to that great commandment are almost certain to live longer than people who don't, because they have freed themselves from deadly negative influences like anger, hatred, suspicion, jealousy, guilt, and anxiety that upset body rhythms and can actually cause organic illness. Such people have more vitality, more resistance to disease, more curiosity, more eagerness, more energy. As the

Book of Isaiah puts it: 'They that wait upon the Lord shall renew their strength; they shall mount up with wings as eagles; they shall run, and not be weary; and they shall walk, and not faint' (40:31).

Another thing that keeps many spiritually minded people going long beyond the average life expectancy is their feeling that God has a reason for their continued existence, even though often they are not quite sure what that reason is.

In the village of Carmel, New York, there a remarkable man named Mort Cheshire. He lived for over 103 years, and he never lost his enthusiasm. Mort was a professional expert in the use of a musical device that has almost become extinct—he played the bones. They were a great favorite in the old-time minstrel shows that I remember as a boy. Mort was famous in old-time vaudeville.

One of the last times I saw Mort, he had reached the ultraripe old age of 102. We were at a Christmas party of the employees of *Guideposts* magazine, which is published in Carmel, New York. Mort was called upon to play the bones. He stood up and played with such enthusiasm and gusto that everyone clapped and cheered and there were even people wiping away tears. Why tears? Because the crowd knew that this proud and remarkable old man still had a firm grip on things. He hadn't quit. He hadn't given in. He had accepted the gift of life and he was still giving something back. Making his cheerful, lively music, he transmitted something wonderful to the crowd of onlookers. We all felt it.

I remember saying to Mort, 'You're terrific! Now tell me, why are you a hundred and two years old and still so vital?'

❧

*It's not how old
you are that
matters; it's how
you are old.*

Marie Dressler

❧

He said, quite simply, 'Because that's what Jesus wants me to be. He must still have some purpose for me here on earth. That's why I'm here.'

He died at 103½, still strong in the faith. How did he do it? He did it because God gave him the gift of the Plus Factor, that's how.

I hear of people like Mort Cheshire frequently. In 1908, for example, Martine Tompkins of Owensboro, Kentucky, became an instant celebrity when she drove down the main street in a Stevens-Duryea touring car. Today, nearly eight decades later, she's still a legend in Owenaboro for her perfect driving record, no violations ever. Someone asked her when she might give up driving. 'When I'm old!' said Martine Tompkins tartly. When she said that, she was only ninety-four.

One thing is certain: The Plus Factor will never fail you just because you're getting old. Let me tell you about another ninety-four-year-old, Effie Ford, who lived all alone in a suburb of Richmond, Virginia. Late one afternoon she decided to walk down to the end of her driveway and take the newspaper, *The News Leader*, out of her mailbox. It was at the end of October; the weatherman had predicted freezing temperatures before morning. Effie wore a thin housedress and a sweater that she had wrapped around her shoulders for the quick trip.

But it wasn't a quick trip. Near the end of the driveway Effie's heel caught in the gravel, and she fell. When she tried to get up, she found that her knees, weakened by arthritis, would not support her. Painfully, the rough concrete scraping her knees and elbows, she managed to drag herself to her own back door. But then she was too weak to get up the steps.

It was about five o'clock; the short autumn afternoon was dying. She called for help. Nobody heard her. Temperatures were dropping rapidly. She tried to cover herself with the doormat at the foot of the steps, but it did little good. Headlights flashed as cars passed by her driveway. But no cars turned in. She felt the warmth of her body draining away into the cold ground.

The hours passed, each one darker and colder and lonelier than the one before. Ninety-four-year-old Effie Ford felt the stealthy languor creeping over her that is the prelude to death from hypothermia. It would have been easy just to accept this, to relax, to go to sleep forever. But something in Effie Ford—that power we call the Plus Factor—would not allow her to give in. She began to twist her body and kick her legs, trying to keep warm. She would count aloud as she kicked, five times with the right leg, five times with the left. She wondered if it were God's will that she should die like this, alone and almost helpless. She decided it was not. She decided God wanted her to fight as long as there was a spark of life in her.

So this daughter of a coal miner, who had raised seven children and endured hardship all her life, refused to give in. All night long, sometimes only half-conscious, she kept fighting. At seven the next morning, a neighbor was horrified to look out his window and see the old lady lying on the ground. He rushed to her side, brought blankets, called an ambulance. And Effie Ford survived.

An incredulous doctor said to her, 'Mrs. Ford, I'll never understand how you survived that freezing night all alone.'

Effie Ford smiled. 'I wasn't alone,' she said. She meant that God was with her . . . and God's gift to people facing almost hopeless odds—the Plus Factor.

I'm sure that this hidden reservoir of power that saved Effie Ford exists in all of us. A well-known doctor said: 'If tension and conflict can be removed from the mind by enlightened self-analysis, and if muscle tension can be removed by a conscious effort to relax the body, then the psychic energy latent in all of us is unchained, and the results are in-creased creativity, a sense of physical well-being, and general enthusiasm for living.'

The psychic energy latent in all of us . . . what is that but the Plus Factor? You can't see or touch it. You can't measure or analyze it. But it's definitely there, waiting to be summoned forth in a crisis, as was the case with Effie Ford.

Older people can accomplish astonishing things, and so can you as the years begin to mount up. I'm sure the good Lord put exactly the same amount of latent Plus Factor into each one of us. Some people are better at activating it than others, that's all.

Here are a handful of suggestions that I've drawn out of my own experience that may help in this business of growing older.

One: Stop looking over your shoulder.

Some older people seem always to be reaching back into the past. It's good to have pleasant memories and okay to go back to them in memory occasionally, but don't stay there. It's much better to face forward, to focus on the future and all the exciting opportunities that it holds. Remember, the advice of the great black baseball player Satchel Paige, who remained a star athlete far longer than the average player. 'Don't look back,' Satchel Paige, used to say, 'somethin' may be gamin' on you.' He didn't say what that 'somethin' was, but he might have meant the regrets and mistakes that are better left behind and forgotten. Live in the now with zest.

Two: Keep elasticity in your attitudes.

Don't let them harden like cement. The world changes. Customs change. Ideas change. You need to retain enough flexibility to change with them. This doesn't mean you have to abandon your basic principles. It just means that you need to let fresh ideas into your mind. Listen to different points of view. Expose yourself to opinions with which you don't necessarily agree. Read books that will push back the boundaries of your mind.

Recently I heard a businessman described like this: 'He has a steel-trap mind, all right, but it snapped shut years ago.' Try not to be like that! Hold on to your tried and true values. If they are of the truth, they are ageless.

Three: Expect health, not helplessness.

As one grows older, it becomes very easy to say, 'Oh, I can't do this; it's too late.' Or, 'I can't try that because I'm too old.' I am sure of one thing: If you expect poor health, if you think poor health, if you proclaim poor health, that is what you are going to have. If on the other hand you see yourself as vigorous and energetic regardless of age, that is the way you are very likely to be. As Oliver Wendell Holmes said, to be seventy years young is sometimes far more cheerful and hopeful than to be forty years old. He was absolutely right. Affirm health, affirm well-being.

Four: Don't say yes to loneliness.

A lot of people do that as they grow older. Their friends die off or drift away and they make no attempt to replace them with new friends. They never volunteer for activities that would bring them into contact with people. They seem to grow more isolated and solitary as the years go by. And more unhappy as they do.

But you don't have to be like that! Loneliness is primarily a state of mind, and the curious, eager, interested mind seldom has time for boredom or room for self-pity. One of the surest antidotes for loneliness is to look around for someone who has troubles and try to help them.

Five: Don't take leave of your senses.

I'm not writing about mental faculties so much as the five basic senses that the good God gave to all of us. How long is it since you brought a fresh-cut rose close to your nostrils and smelled that incredible fragrance? How long is it since you went out at night and looked—really looked—at the stars? How long since you listened to the music and magic of poetry read aloud, or to the murmur of the surf on a lonely beach? How long since you tasted hot home-made bread fresh from the oven? How long since you scuffed your way, ankle deep, through the gold and crimson leaves of autumn? Or smelled the scent of wood smoke? Or heard the wild calling of Canada geese passing across the face of the harvest moon? Too long, probably.

It may be true that some senses like eyesight or hearing grow less keen with the passing years, but usually you can rectify that. Get a magnifying glass and study the composition of a piece of quartz or the texture of a flower. Turn the volume up a little on your favorite recording; if the neighbors complain, invite them in to listen. Get up early some morning and watch the sun come up; you don't need reading glasses to watch the miracle of a sunrise.

Don't take leave of your senses just because you're older. And don't let your senses take leave of you.

Six: Live your life forgetting age.

An eighty-six-year-old friend was the owner and manager of a big hotel in Chicago. With admiration I watched him supervising a dinner of 1,500 people where I was the speaker. 'Frank,' I asked, 'how old are you anyway?' 'What's the matter? Isn't your room okay, the service here satisfactory?' 'Well, I know how old you are for you went to school with my mother.'

'Listen, son,' he said—and that 'son' went over big with me. 'Live your life and forget your age.' Then he told me that when he looked into a mirror, he didn't see Frank Bering, an old man. He saw Frank Bering— period.

Seven: Don't ever retire from living.

I warn you that the Plus Factor will begin to desert you if you do. Keep your capacity for wonder alive. Keep in touch with the amazing and astounding world around you. Keep trying new things. You're never too old to be creative. We're told that Titian painted *The Battle of Lepanto* when he was 98, and Verdi composed the soaring music of *Aida* when he was in his 80s. Goethe and Tolstoy did some of their best work in their later years. Most of us can never be such towering geniuses. But it's possible to remain creative as long as you live. Remember this great fact:

If you don't give up on life, life won't give up on you.

Eight: Enjoy being yourself.

Dr. Hans Selye, the great expert on stress, said that most emotional stress is caused by trying to be something you're not. Older people can usually stop worrying about what the Joneses think. They can express opinions freely. They don't have to conform so much. They don't have to be so aggressive, so striving, so materialistic in their outlook on life. They have more time, and sometimes more inclination, to help other people. Your later years can be a very pleasant and productive time—if you can find the serenity that comes from just being yourself.

Nine: Live a day at a time.

View each day as precious. Live it to the full. Skip any idea that 'you're running out of time.' Take every day and its abundance of opportunity and make the most of it. You'll be surprised at what you can do.

I spoke to a big dinner of over 2,500 people along with General Jimmy Doolittle. General Doolittle, one of our greatest American heroes, won the Congressional Medal of Honor for leading sixteen bombers in 1942 on America's first bombing raid against Japan. It was one of the most heroic exploits in American history.

The general, now at ninety years of age, thrilled the vast crowd at that dinner with his speech. Asked how he handled age, he replied, 'I do just what I've always done. I live one day at a time.' And I might add, his Plus Factor seems to be working as well as it always has.

19

Keeping the Plus Factor Going

To keep the Plus Factor going I suggest doing this:

Incorporate into your thought pattern and life-style the ten golden attitudes. They are:

> Faith
> Positive Thinking
> Persistence
> Confidence
> Positive Imaging
> Prayer
> Affirmation
> Belief
> Love
> Work

They do not necessarily need to be in the order listed above. But if all ten, or even a majority of these attitudes, are employed regularly, the result will be that the special quality called the Plus Factor will be kept going in you always. And your life will thereby be filled with joy and satisfaction and achievement.

I have been teaching and advocating this way of life for quite some years. And I have received many messages from persons in nearly every section of the world telling that they have applied these principles and that they have worked successfully. Many of these communications have borne enthusiastic testimony that the incorporation of the ten golden attitudes have turned lives around and led people to a quality of success and happiness they never dreamed of attaining.

So in this final chapter I want to explore just how these attitudes which I have chosen to call 'golden' have worked successfully in the experience of so many individuals.

The first person I wish to tell you about exemplifies the positive effect of creative discontent. He was a New York City taxi driver who drove me to Kennedy Airport. His cab was spotlessly clean—immaculate—as was the driver himself. This man had a streak of genius, for not only was he contented—he was also discontented. But he told me right off that he was a confirmed positive thinker.

While driving along, the radio news gave a brief rundown on a speech made the night before by the governor. It was an impassioned declaration that he, the governor, was committed to driving all rats out of New York City.

The driver flipped off the radio saying, 'I don't know whether the governor knows how to get rid of rats. But I do. In fact, I used to live in a ghetto section of Manhattan. But,' he declared, 'there were never any rats in my house.'

'How come?' I asked.

'Because our house was clean, spotlessly clean. And I mean clean. My wife is a terrific housekeeper. She hates dirt and so there just wasn't any dirt in our place. It doesn't make any difference how poor a neighborhood may be, there is no excuse for your own house not being clean. And there is another way to outsmart rats,' he told me. 'I just filled any kind of opening with shattered glass. That makes it so tough for a rat that it gets discouraged and bypasses your place.

'Even in a so-called ghetto neighborhood I was a contented man,' he smiled broadly, 'and why not: lovely wife, good kids, and a nice home? What more could you ask? I was a contented man and a positive thinker . . .

'But . . .' and then came good old creative discontent. 'I wanted something better: a house out of town with grass and trees and flowers. So I worked hard and saved my money and one of my passengers, an investment man, gave me an idea on how to invest the little I had and what do you know?'

'Okay, what?' I asked, fascinated by this story of good old American self-reliance. Well, he got his house—on Long Island. It had a few scraggly trees and a beat-up lawn and no flowers. The man knew nothing about how to make a lawn or grow flowers. But he got some pamphlets on flower and grass culture. And a Sunday newspaper supplement gave him tips on gardening. Eventually he had a lawn and a garden that was the talk of the neighborhood. So much so that all the envious housewives on the street pressured their husbands to get to work gardening. An entire neighborhood was transformed into a place of beauty.

'Wonderful,' I said, 'positively wonderful! Isn't it something—what a human being can do when really motivated by contentment powered by discontent? Someone who doesn't wait for a government housing program but who gets along on his own.

'So now you're really contented, I'm sure.'

'Sure I am,' he replied proudly. 'I'm a contented man. Lovely wife, good kids, beautiful home and garden . . . but . . .'

He started telling me what was on his drawing board for the future, and it sounded mighty like driving discontent for something better.

That this New York City cab driver has his Plus Factor in top working order was obvious. The next time I have the good fortune to ride in his taxi he may have some harsh experiences to tell me about, but that he will also be able to tell of his victories over them I have no doubt. For he is the sort of man who rolls with the punches and comes out a winner. And the creative discontent that prods him always to something better is one of the reasons.

Now let me tell you of one of my inspiring friends, Pete McCulley, quarterback coach of the Kansas City Chiefs of the National Football League. He had been, successively, receiver coach with the Baltimore Colts and Washington Redskins. Then he attained his dream and goal by becoming head coach of the San Francisco 49ers in the eighteenth year of his highly successful professional coaching career. Then the devastating blow came. He was let go from this athletically exalted position.

Twelve ways to grow bigger
within yourself.
Pray big. Think big.
Believe big. Act big.
Dream big. Work big.
Give big. Forgive big.
Laugh big. Image big.
Love big. Live big.

But despite this shock and adversity, Pete McCulley's Plus Factor was working magnificently. Ed Jacoubowsky, sportswriter for the *Palo Alto Times* said of him, 'But McCulley exits with dignity. "I'm not going to blame anyone but me," he says. "You're either successful or you can't stay around in this business. You can't go through life blaming others.

' "You hope when you get a chance in the NFL—that's the ultimate in coaching—you just hope things work out better than this.

' "But it's history," he concludes, "It's done with, it's over."

'Maybe for some people, but not for Pete McCulley. Whatever he does, he'll be successful. He's a winner.'

As one of the most qualified coaches in professional football, he soon landed a top coaching job with the New York Jets. It was then that he wrote me the following letter. It is the letter of a real champion with a big Plus Factor going for him. And as you will see from this communication, he knows how to keep it going. He practices the ten golden attitudes. Well, here is the letter:

Dear Dr. Peale:

Two years ago when we moved to Long Island to accept a coaching position with the New York Jets, I felt as if I left my heart in San Francisco. I had been released as head coach of the San Francisco 49ers after attaining my career dream of being a head coach of a National Football League team. It was like swallowing a square pill and my morale was so low that I felt like I would have to dig up to get to the bottom.

However, the New York move was a blessing because it located me in an area where one of God's own could provide positive aid for a wounded spirit.

As a coach, I have experienced numerous victories over every kind of defeat and difficulty. In fact ordinarily when I fall in a mud hole, I check my hip pocket to see if I've caught a fish. However, in this case I needed a good dose of your practical approach to Christianity for a full recovery and peace of mind.

Recently I have been toughening up my physical and spiritual muscles in my foxhole. My foxhole is located in our basement where I have weight-lifting equipment, an indoor bicycle and a tape recorder. In addition, I have at least thirty of your sermons on tape. Each morning at 6:00 A.M. when I work out, I listen to two of your tapes in my effort to hone my physical and spiritual muscles at the same time. In athletics, it is said, fatigue makes cowards of all that compete for a high goal. I believe this applies to the spiritual as well and I certainly don't want to get fatigued and fall short of the goal.

Thanks for providing the fuel to flame the hungry kind of feelings that burn deep inside of me to find God's will in a meaningful life. It is indeed as promised, the victory that 'overcometh the world.' God bless you every day.

Sincerely,

Pete McCulley

Currently Pete has an assistant coaching job at Kansas City. Through his strong faith and mature understanding of the ups and downs in football as in life itself Pete McCulley has become a great positive thinker. He knows that positive thinking works when the going is good and that it also works when the going gets rough. And that to meet life situations masterfully is what the ten golden attitudes help us to do.

In fact, a major ability we must cultivate is how to react when the rough times come. These golden attitudes are not designed to make life a bed of roses, but rather to toughen us up to meet and handle trouble and difficulty like strong men and women. The constant and sincere use of those ten principles stated on the opening page of the chapter will make life better, even great, and will lead to real success. But they will also give strong sustaining power when the hard knocks come. They will, in fact, pull you through anything and get you going again even when everything seems hopeless. So say the many persons who have communicated with me.

Scheduled to speak to a public meeting of sales people in Pittsburgh one night, I entered by the stage door and sat backstage waiting for the program to begin. A rather stocky athletic-looking man came back and introduced himself as the master of ceremonies for the meeting. He was an animated person, full of vigor and enthusiasm. His positive attitude came through impressively.

He told me he had been a helicopter pilot in the war in South-east Asia. Shot down, he was so seriously wounded that his life was despaired of. Because of suspected brain damage, doctors came to a tentative diagnosis that if he did live it would 'be as a vegetable.' He underwent a brain operation that left a small plate in the top of his head. Moved to a military hospital in the United States, he was paralyzed in both legs and both arms. His speech, however, was not affected nor was his mental ability.

One day he said to his wife, 'Bring a book I once read about positive thinking and read it to me.' Day after day, his wife read about the powerful creative and recreative principles of positive thinking until this desperately wounded man developed an extraordinary positive attitude.

Then came the conviction that he, too, could be healed despite the disheartening prognosis.

He told his wife that he was going to reprogram his mind to take charge of his broken body. He entered upon an intensive and persistent routine of positive thinking and spiritual affirmation, infusing his mind with a powerful directive force. His eventual healing did not come in a miraculous way, nor did it come all that easily; but that it did come was evidenced by the physically strong and mentally alert man who told me this story of what a motivated human being can do with himself when his faith is strong enough in content and force. He knew how to keep his Plus Factor going.

Later as I watched this remarkable man emcee the meeting with humor and spirit that set a positive and enthusiastic tone, I once again reaffirmed my own certain belief that an in-depth positive attitude wins over all difficulties. So keep it going—always keep it going. Miracles are built into persons who program their mind to in-depth belief.

Even deteriorating marriages based on the golden attitudes program reverse themselves and do well, as the following letter illustrates. It is from a lady in Australia, where I have spoken on several occasions.

Dear Dr. Peale:

I managed to get two tickets in the last row for your meeting and talked my husband into taking me, because I wanted him to hear your positive ideas.

My husband has been a very negative and anxiety prone person, coming from a large family without any love or affection. We have been married nearly thirty years and have five children and up until now my husband was not a very good husband or father, nor was he a success financially. He had a heart-attack three years ago but thank God he recovered.

I picked up a copy of your book *The Power of Positive Thinking* and decided to put into practice some of the principles in your book and a miracle has happened in our marriage. We are closer now than we have been for nearly twenty years. My husband has become the person he should have been all these years.

Thank you for helping me to look at my God in a more positive way. I am a Catholic but the idea of taking him into partnership with me had never occurred to me, and I know we could not have repaired our lives without His help.

We enjoyed your lecture so much. The hall seemed to be filled with your presence. I hope you are spared for many years to do God's work in this present time. I am,

Yours sincerely,

Several references in her letter indicate that this lady is a practitioner of the ten golden principles or attitudes. In times of difficulty she has moved through to victory. The Plus Factor within, coupled with faith and prayer and positive thinking, has been her secret all the way.

One should never face a difficult problem negatively. Never assume that nothing can be done about it. The first thing to do is to think. Practically every problem is solvable if we think coolly, objectively, and intellectually. Never give in to emotionalizing. Instead, think and pray and affirm that the power, the insight, the wisdom is given you to handle this troublesome situation. Affirm by saying, 'I have a Plus Factor in me. It is now coming to my aid in power so that I am well able to handle this problem.'

Then summon your faith to aid you. Remember always that great promise, 'If you have faith as a mustard seed, you will say to this mountain [this difficulty], 'Move from here to there,' and it will move; and nothing will be impossible for you.'

In this superlative manner the Plus Factor that was built into us by the Creator and the ten golden attitudes given to us work together. Thus the problems of life are solved, overcome, or lived with victoriously. By consistent affirmation you are firmly fixing the success image in consciousness; you are in effect praying the powerful prayer of faith. And this quality of high-level prayer overcomes because it is indicative of faith. Remember the promise 'According to your faith be it done unto you.'

In addition to the activation of the inherent Plus Factor and the development of the power to keep it going, those ten golden attitudes are of prime importance. Look carefully at them again:

Faith

Positive Thinking

Persistence

Confidence

Positive Imaging

Prayer

Affirmation

Belief

Love

Work

In my opinion, which is based on thousands of personal cases over many years, the best way by far to get out of trouble and to have a creative and happy life is to live by the ten golden attitudes. I mean this not only sincerely, but also enthusiastically. This way of life will release your own native personal abilities as nothing else can. Your plus power will produce ideas one after the other which will contribute to your ability to handle things more successfully. I've seen it work in the experience of too many people of all types and backgrounds to have the slightest vestige of doubt about the truth of what I am writing here.

The experiences which have been related in this chapter bear out the fact that the teachings of Jesus Christ produce the best values in life and endow the believer with the ability to meet and overcome even the most difficult problems. I am not saying that they will produce riches and give a person everything he wants, for what he may want cannot be assumed to be what God wants for him. But I am saying that his needs will be fulfilled and God in His great generosity will provide him with His good in full measure.

I have always noted that those people who not only follow the teachings of Jesus but who also possess His spirit of love, compassion, and esteem for others have their own Plus Factor always going with extra force.

An old friend, Ben Sweetland, a well-known writer, was respected and loved by many. He was a positive personality who loved to help individuals. And he often performed such help in innovative ways. How he activated the Plus Factor in a house painter is a story he told me over dinner one evening in San Francisco.

Ben was having some painting done in his home by a man named John Doyce, who one day said, 'You're so lucky. How I would love to have my own home!' Knowing that the painter was about forty-five years old and married, Ben asked him why he didn't. John then proceeded to recite a long list of the expenses involved in raising two children in a time of an ever-increasing cost of living. He just about came out even.

Ben left John to his painting, but later in the day came back with a box in his hand. It was a simple candy box that Ben had transformed into a makeshift bank. He asked for a coin. Puzzled, the painter pulled a dime out of his pocket, which Ben took and dropped into the slot in the 'bank.' He then handed over the box saying, 'John, you're on your way to owning your own home.'

John looked surprised, but Ben explained that he needed to establish the habit of saving. Every time he earned any money, he was to take some part of it, no matter how small, and put it in the box. Ultimately, the dribs and drabs would amount to something. The painter took the 'bank' with him, but Ben could see he was dubious about the whole thing.

A few years later, though, Ben received in the mail an invitation to a housewarming—from John and his wife. The home was not simply adequate, but charming and imaginative.

John told Ben that it wasn't the saving of the money that was the most important factor in the building of the house—and in other areas of his life as well, It was learning to change his attitude—replacing 'I can't' with 'I can.' Once he saw his savings overflow the candy box into a bank account, he took on extra jobs and put the whole amount earned from them into the 'building fund.' Persuading John to take that all-important first step, Ben Sweetland helped to activate his Plus Factor. A change in attitude kept it going.

To help anyone to realize that 'he can' instead of 'he can't' is actually an act of love. For by so doing you are activating and releasing that extra talent, that greater something that the Creator placed in that person. To care enough for people to assist them to be what they can be is a high form of Christian practice. And further to do something that will aid another person in keeping his Plus Factor going and developing is to add to his success and happiness and to your own also.

As I come to the closing pages of this book, I find myself remembering a little church in Switzerland and some words I heard spoken there.

One Sunday in Zermatt my wife, Ruth, and I went to the little English church that stands in the heart of the village. Conducting services that morning was a bishop of the Church of England, tall, stately, white-haired, with long, expressive, blue-veined hands. He read from the prayer book in his correct British intonation, each syllable as clear and distinct as a fresh-minted coin. Finally he closed the book, came down from the pulpit, stood in the aisle, and said he would just like to talk to us informally for a few minutes. And what he had to say was memorable indeed.

He told us about the little cemetery in the center of the village where some of the climbers are buried who lost their battle with the great Matterhorn. On some of the graves, he said, you can see the ice-axes that belonged to these brave men. Then he asked some questions. 'Why are you here today? Why am I here? We may have lesser reasons, but our true reason for being here, whether we're aware of it or not, is to have fellowship with the mountains.' He quoted the majestic words from Psalm 121: "I will lift up mine eyes unto the hills, from whence cometh my help.' 'A hush fell over the congregation as he spoke. One could feel the quiet strength of the great mountains enfolding us, stealing into our hearts, bringing peace and tranquility and a deep awareness of the mighty Power that had called those mountains into existence.

The bishop pointed to the church wall. 'Do you see that plaque over there? To me it's not merely a plaque; it's a boy who lies in the graveyard. An English boy. I knew him well. I knew his parents. The boy came here when he was only twenty-one. He was climbing the Matterhorn eagerly, confidently, when a rope broke and he fell . . .'

The bishop stopped speaking. All around us the hush seemed to deepen.

Finally the bishop spoke again. 'But was that the end for this young lad so full of life and promise? Those who knew him don't think so. His parents don't

245

think so. I don't think so. In that graveyard where he lies with the others there is a sentence carved in stone that says, 'In the sight of the unwise, they seem to die.' Death is the illusion; the shortsighted view. Those with more wisdom know that this boy died climbing. He was moving up. And in the life beyond this life he is still moving up, he is climbing still. . .'

Again the bishop paused. There was not a sound in the little church. Finally he went on, 'And so I say to you, when you go forth from this place, find a mountain to climb. Find a difficulty and overcome it. Find an obstacle and master it. All around you are the great life-giving, life-sustaining forces of the universe. Give yourself to them. Trust them. Lift up your eyes to the hills. Keep them fixed on the highest peaks . . . and you will always find the strength you need.'

Ruth and I left that church inspired and uplifted. Wherever you are, whoever you are, have faith in God. Experience the life-changing power of Jesus Christ. Develop your God-given Plus Factor. Do these things and you can live magnificently and handle creatively anything life brings to you.

□□□

Secrets of Success

Charles Newton

When was the last time you tried to punch a hole in the sky?

Tests Pilots, punching into stratosphere, climbing to undreamt heights in jets and rocket planes, have a phrase they use to describe their work.

They call it 'punching holes in the sky.'

That is what we are meant to do with our lives, to climb beyond the humdrum, to reach beyond the preoccupation of daily existence. However, more often that not, we aim too low. When it comes to living we settle for the mediocre. We are human, we tell ourselves. The sky is too high to think of. It is the impossible that stops us. But nonetheless it is the challenge of the impossible that gets life out of its rut and onto a highway that leads us to our goal.

Think big, work hard and have the courage to dream. Make the impossible your goal.

Remember, if you don't care for your dreams, who will.

Whatever your personals goals, this book will help you become the person you have always wanted to be.

"... a delectable book which in irresistible prose lays down the keys to success."

— Amrita Bazar Patrika.

Practical Ways to a Powerful Personality

Dr. George Weinberg

An impressive and powerful personality is an essential asset for each one of us today. In this useful and highly acclaimed book, Dr. Weinberg, a practising psychotherapist, shows how by a judicious choice of correct actions, we can rid our personalities of fear, anxiety and shame. He illustrates his ideas with numerous examples and suggests practical ways to develop a powerful personality.

"A reading delight as well as a source of help for personal problem solving."

— Los Angeles Times, U.S.A.

"Stimulating and valuable...."

— Kirkus Bulletin, U.S.A.

"A book that everyone must read...."

— M.P. Chronicle

"Widely acclaimed.... a classic!"

— Pioneer

Available at all bookshops or by V.P.P.

Orient Paperbacks

Madarsa Road, Kashmere Gate, Delhi-110 006